SAVVY

Second Edition

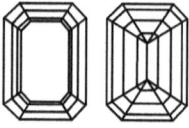

emerald

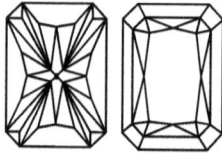

radiant Sq

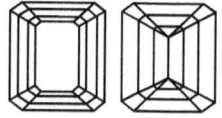

ashcher

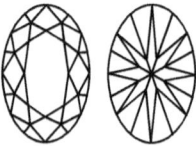

oval

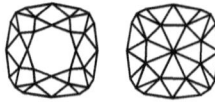

cushion

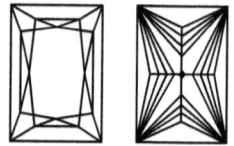

princess

marquise

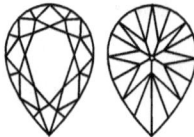

pearose

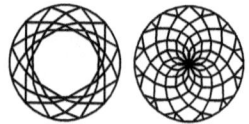

spiral

SAVVY

Become a Jewelry & Gemstone Connoisseur...Overnight!

Second Edition

Christine Cameron

Published by Dreamcatchers Dawn
Las Vegas, Nevada

DEDICATION

This Second Edition of SAVVY is dedicated to my friends and colleagues, especially those who have offered both their constructive criticism and support of the first book. Their desire to know more...as well as to encourage my success...has prompted me to improve upon the first edition of SAVVY with this second version. Within these additional thirty pages, I hope to have made them proud and to have also contributed to their growing interest in the expansive world of exotic gemstones. As with fine wine, by gleaning continual knowledge and understanding, their tastes in jewelry should also evolve and refine over time...and I certainly hope I play a major role in their on-going edification of fine jewels.

And, as always, I must commend my wonderful husband, Lynn. His unwavering support, keen insight, and blinding brilliance enable me everyday. With his regular TLC and subtle, persistent polishing, I am continually encouraged to display my inner luster to the world. Thank you, my stellar twin! I love you.

Christine

ACKNOWLEDGMENTS

This handy guide has been created for all those high-jewelry lovers who wish they had a trusted gem expert available at any time to answer their questions. Drawing upon years of experience, Christine suggests tricks of the trade to help you navigate the sometimes overwhelming world of exotic gemstones. Study Christine's insider tips then confidently purchase your next exquisite piece as a savvy jewelry connoisseur.

This easy read is meant to be a quick reference for those wanting to know the right questions to ask and what to look for when shopping for fine jewelry. It's not intended to be a compendium of all knowledge or all information about the world of gemology. That would (and does) take countless books on the subject.

SAVVY simply, and in layman's terms, covers the most poignant and common scenarios you'll find when shopping for luxury jewelry and exotic gemstones. Should you negotiate price? How do you know the stone is all that the salesperson claims it is? How will you know it's a quality piece? Does it have true intrinsic value? What color should it really be? You'll be able to answer all these questions - and more - by the end of this book as Christine guides you through the most popular gems in today's marketplace.

Be savvy and shop with confidence, secure that you have industry insight within these pages to help you source the crème de la crème of exotic and luxury jewels.

Christine Cameron

savvyswagbag.com

Swag Bag Party
Personalized Trunk Shows
Designer Discounts
And More…

Your Discount Code: **2SAVVY**

swag@savvyswagbag.com

CONTENTS

LIST OF APPENDICES

INTRODUCTION

Market Trends Update

As we stated in the original edition of SAVVY, **we are not licensed to, nor do we assume to, give you any financial advice regarding investments or gem purchases**. The statements made in SAVVY are based purely on modern gemstone market trends and from observing the prices of certain scarce gems as their worth continues to increase over the years…especially as those particular stones become more and more rare. Simply put: the value of these jewels typically continues to surge as the availability of these gems steadily decreases. It's basic supply and demand for gemstones that become harder and harder to obtain.

Later in this guide, beginning on page 56 under the heading *Collector Stones*, we offer a listing of gemstones that we know many gem aficionados strive to add to their collections. Based on market observations, these particular gems have continued to go up in monetary value over the past several years. Why? Because they're becoming more and more scarce and are more difficult to find in good quality and/or in sufficient quantity.

In an effort to keep our readers up-to-date on the latest industry and gemstone trends, we're highlighting a few gems here that jewelry aficionados may want to consider adding to their collections. By our own in-house categorization, these gems currently fall under the "scarce" category, and we suggest that you grab them if you can. Why? Because the stones mentioned below will, in the foreseeable future, and in all likelihood, become gems that have gone from scarce to rare. When scarce gems move into the "rare" category, their monetary and market values tend to skyrocket within a very short period of time. In fact, the gemstones itemized below are already increasing in value (and price) as we type this introduction.

PINK DIAMONDS – specifically from the Argyle mine in Australia.

Reason: the Argyle diamond mine in Australia is the primary source of high quality, fancy pink diamonds on the planet. This mine currently produces over 90% of the world's fancy pink diamonds, and it also yields the *highest quality* pink diamonds found anywhere on the globe. These luscious pinks are naturally colored by Mother Earth; and to give you an understanding of the rarity of these incredible jewels, you need to realize just how unusual they are: at the Argyle mine, out of approximately every one million carats of diamond rough, only *one* carat is considered a quality fancy pink! These ultra-fine pinks are so rare that they can garner over $100,000 per carat; and depending upon the intensity of the saturation of color (how rich and jewel-toned the hue), they can glean upwards of $1million per carat.

Why buy now? Because it has been forecasted that the Argyle diamond mine may slow production of these incredible gems by 2019. The mine is constructed as an open pit, and it has become incredibly deep…so deep that there are now concerns and considerations on whether the mine can continue its operation. In layman's terms, this mine, for all intents and purposes, could soon be closed (until such time as new technologies are invented or underground mining passages become operational). As this paragraph is being typed (Summer 2013), an underground passage is planned to come online; but it is yet to be seen how much product it will yield. So when, and if, this mine does close for good, the supply of the world's highest quality fancy pink diamonds will dry up overnight. These already scarce jewels will certainly become rare; and natural fancy pink diamonds with their origins in the Kimberly region of Australia will undoubtedly soar in value instantly. In fact, because of the anticipation that the mine may indeed close in just a few short years, the prices of pink diamonds worldwide are now, a few years out, already on a steep rise.

Of interest, the Argyle mine recently yielded three ultra-rare, natural, fancy red diamonds and three incredible natural fancy blues – the likes of which are rarely seen on Earth! There continues to be a demonstrable and proven reason why the Argyle mine in Australia is considered to produce the best quality fancy color diamonds on the planet.

CEYLON BLUE SAPPHIRE – the best blue you can find.

Reason: color sapphires, particularly the ones that are the perfect shade of royal blue, are currently harder to come by. At the time of this writing (Summer 2013), a high quality royal blue (Ceylon blue) sapphire can garner upwards of $3,000 per carat at *wholesale*. There are a variety of factors contributing to the current blue sapphire craze, but one of the main reasons is that active mines around the world are not yielding what they once did. Thus, a shortage of quality gems – mixed with growing demand around the globe – is producing a blue sapphire frenzy; and whenever these perfectly colored royal blue sapphires do hit the market, they're grabbed up instantly.

Of interest, high quality blue sapphires historically have been great jewels to include in any collection. They typically retain their worth; and in times of scarcity, they escalate in value. When certain sapphires from specific mines become rare, as with the now infamous and revered Kashmir sapphires, their intrinsic value rises exponentially to the point where, today, they are priceless. Kashmir sapphires truly are crown jewels, and they are the epitome of museum quality gemstones.

Regarding precious gemstones, you cannot go wrong investing

in a high quality, perfectly colored Ceylon (royal blue) sapphire. And of course, natural, <u>not</u> heat treated, is best.

IMPERIAL "CHAMPAGNE" GARNET – a newer find, possibly a different variety of Imperial Malaia Garnet from Madagascar?

Reason: the "imperial champagne garnet" that we refer to here is a dichroic pyrope-spessartine garnet that was discovered in a small pocket in Africa in 2011. Since this particular garnet comes from a small find, it is anticipated that these brownish pinkish orange, aka. "champagne," garnets will sell out quickly.

For those of you not familiar with the dynamic and colorful family of exotic garnets, this "imperial champagne" stone, like many of its nesosilicate cousins, could conceivably jump in value very quickly. If it follows its family trend, the "imperial champagne garnet" will be a find for any collector. Take, for example, its amazingly brilliant, sun-colored cousin, the mandarin garnet. Mandarin garnet, found in Africa, has been one of the fastest appreciating gemstones in modern history. In fact, mandarin garnets of good tangerine color are now becoming rare, and their value has subsequently gone through the roof! Similarly, another cousin, the esteemed, elusive and exotic Russian demantoid garnet, with its eye-catching and piercing green light display, when found in high quality, garners more money per carat than diamonds! In fact, the Russian demantoid garnet is more rare and is equally as brilliant as a fancy diamond. And then there is the popular and refreshing Tsavorite garnet. It's a single-source gem, with its origins in Kenya, whose flow to market is tightly controlled. Tsavorite garnets are not too common with American retailers, yet they are stunning – as richly green and crystal clean as a jungle after a refreshing downpour – and they are rarely found in sizes larger than two carats. Currently, there's a dispute in ownership over the Tsavorite mine – and therefore, the flow of these verdant gems has slowed to the marketplace – and thus, it's easy to see why the value of Tsavorite garnets continues to increase. Then there are other garnet cousins, such as the Arizona Anthill garnet. It's a beautiful, rich wine-red gem, and it has become popular among gem aficionados because of how it's mined: ants…yes, those pesky little insects, ants…move the garnet rough to the surface of the ground while they're busy burrowing and building their mounds. Whenever they encounter a garnet stone underground and it impedes the building of their anthill, they'll hoist the gem up and out of the mound, letting it roll away onto the surface of the ground. Thus the name: "anthill garnets." Then the ant-harvested garnets lay on the ground until the Navajo gather them up.

So, if the exotic "imperial champagne garnet" follows in the footsteps of its many dynamic and colorful garnet cousins, this newly discovered gemstone should follow a similar trajectory in popularity and increasing value. Since this unusual gem was first brought to market in 2011, and it is found in only one place in Africa, it's a new treasure. If you're someone who wants to wear something that no one else has, and you desire something that's bound to remain elusive and exotic, the Imperial Champagne Garnet is a gem for you to consider.

CAMBODIAN BLUE ZIRCON – Teal blue perfection!

Reason: its supply out of Cambodia is limited and its popularity is growing. The demand for good quality blue zircon is rising steadily…and in large part because blue zircon is being touted as a popular alternate birthstone for December.

Tanzanite, another popular December birthstone, is directly affecting the demand for blue zircon. Why? Because the price of good tanzanite is dramatically on the rise. Quality tanzanite is harder and harder to find; and with the availability of good tanzanite diminishing (and, consequently, its prices rising), the birthstone demand has switched away from tanzanite and has moved over to blue zircon instead, yet the blue zircon supply remains tight. Meanwhile, more and more people are learning about this stunning teal gem and are wanting to wear it for its dazzling beauty whether they have a December birthday or not. Thus, the prices for the richest, most vibrant Cambodian blue zircon are climbing fast. True, other colors of zircon (and some blue) are also found in Sri Lanka, but it's the Cambodian blue zircon that's known worldwide to produce the deepest, richest shade of teal with the piercing brilliance of a neon laser light show.

Although the mine in the Rattanakiri area of Cambodia, about forty miles from the Cambodian-Vietnamese border, still produces a steady stream of blindingly gorgeous teal blue gems, the increasing popularity and demand for these stones has caused the gems to become more scarce…and, therefore, more expensive.

If you find one you love, grab it! When viewed side-by-side, you'll see why the Cambodian jewel, versus a Sri Lankan stone, is the crowned prince. No other gem produces such a teal that can electrify a room.

HOLD THE PRESSES – DON'T MISS THESE SUPER HOT GEMS!
Siberian Amethyst, Yellow Diamonds, Pakistani Peridot, and Sleeping Beauty Turquoise…

At the very last minute, we've paused the printing of this book to add four more fabulous gems to this list for you. Pay close and quick attention to these jewels: Siberian Amethyst, fancy Yellow Diamonds, Pakistani Peridot, and Sleeping Beauty Turquoise.

These stones, if natural and of good quality, are scalding HOT right now…so hot that it's incumbent upon us to postpone our publishing so that we can include them in this edition for you; we would be remiss if we didn't tell you about these amazing gems in a timely fashion.

In recent weeks/months, each of these particular stones has risen exponentially in cost. Why? For the same reason that many stones see a sudden burst in their values and, consequently, their costs – they are now scarcer than ever before; and some, like the Siberian amethyst and Pakistani peridot, are simply no longer available. The same goes for the exquisite Sleeping Beauty Turquoise. Its mine in Globe, Arizona, is now closed and no more of its immaculate robin-egg blue phosphates can be unearthed. If wholesale gemstone dealers cannot acquire any more of these stones through their sources at the mines, then they have nothing to supply to the retailers. Consequently, the gemstone's availability begins to fall off dramatically at the retail level, and this is when the frenzy starts – the demand for these stones, by reaction, out-paces what's available. Dealers clamor to get their hands on these precious jewels…but they simply cannot find them.

In the last few months, Siberian amethyst have increased more than 700% in price (at the wholesale level)!

Fancy yellow and cognac diamonds are already on the rise, up 30%.

Sleeping Beauty turquoise has already doubled in price at the retail level (if not more) and is anticipated to continue its steady climb.

High quality Pakistani peridot, likewise, is going through the same price spikes.

These newfound market values reflect increasing scarcity as these amazing jewels steadily become more and more rare, especially the ones of high quality and of fabulous color! These four jewels are undoubtedly gems that need to be added to your collection as soon as you come across any that avail themselves to you…and this is why we've halted the presses to tell you.

And, yes, for those of you wondering, the market for jewels can – and often does – move this quickly. With the global demand for colored stones being continually on the rise in recent years, the sudden unavailability of popular gems often causes their prices to spike…and seemingly overnight!

HONORABLE MENTIONS
In addition to the current craze over fancy diamonds, exotic garnets, Siberian amethyst, and Cambodian blue zircon, as always,

there are some extraordinary gemstones that belong in any aficionado's collection. Throughout the years, these gems have remained high on collectors' lists…and for all the right reasons. Some of these 'honorable mention' gems are:

Burmese Rubies
Padparadscha Sapphires
African Copper Bearing Tourmaline
African Chrome Tourmaline
Muzo Mine Emeralds
Rhodochrosite (from the Sweet Home Mine)
Tanzanian Pink Spinel

And, of course, it almost goes without mention…

Kashmir Sapphire
Paraiba Tourmaline
(from Paraiba, Brazil – you should pursue the perfect hue of richest greenish-blue aged copper patina)

The above are suggestions for active collectors who are continuing to expand their repertoires. For those of you just beginning to build your jewelry ensembles, choose the best quality gems you can afford with stones that you love and have an affinity for. Once you've found your favorites, build your collections around exotics, definitely some of the ones mentioned above, and anything else that intrigues you.

Keep in mind, our suggestions are for *quality gems only*. Per evaluation using the "4 C" standards, any of these jewels (if natural and of high quality) should be worth adding to anyone's collection.

1 – THE RIGHT QUESTIONS

Questions to Ask in the Jewelry Store:

1. What is this gemstone?
2. Is this gem natural?
3. Is it lab created?
4. Is it enhanced? If so, how?
5. If applicable, does it come with a lab certification (GIA or EGL preferred)?

Questions to Ask yourself:

1. Do you love the piece?
2. Would you wear it? Or....
3. Would you be proud to give it as a gift?

If you answered "yes" to the questions above, then it's the piece for you. Only one thing is pending before you purchase it: the price.

Pricing Questions:

Q: Can I negotiate the price down?

A: Oftentimes, yes. Many jewelers are accustomed to negotiating or doing a little discounting. It's an inherent part of this age-old industry...and it never hurts to ask.

Some customers instinctively may want to counter whatever price they've just been quoted by the salesperson with a lower counter-offer. That's more than fair, and it's also appropriate. If you try it, you'll learn quickly whether the store is open to negotiations or not. Just wait and see how the salesperson responds.

Some customers also ask (wisely) if there's a special price for a cash payment in full. If you have that cash on hand (or are willing to get it), see how the salesperson responds.

These are fair and reasonable questions to ask. The worst the sales person can say is, "No, we don't negotiate our prices." OK. Fine. Then you know. Incidentally, many stores have adopted payment plans that make it easier and more comfortable for their customers to make the purchase; and sometimes the retailers do this in lieu of negotiating their prices. Some stores allow their clientele to put down a portion of the full price and then make interest-free payments on the balance due over a period of several months. That may make the purchase, especially if it's a large one, more palatable for the customer.

Regarding pricing and negotiations:

1. What are the industry standards?

   a. There are none. Typically, smaller, family-owned retailers are often willing to work with the customer on prices. In international (non-American) locations, many shop owners are open and accustomed to negotiating. However, in the US, many big box, nationwide retailers are much more hesitant. Their business models are more about fixed pricing and rarely, if ever, discounting. Since there are no hard and fast industry rules, and they vary store by store, it never hurts to offer less than the sticker price. You may be surprised at how many jewelers are open to negotiating prices. (It's an age-old tradition that's an inherent part of this industry). Name a reasonable price that you're willing to pay, and see how the jeweler responds. If the jeweler counters your offer with some concession on price or payment plans, you're off to a good negotiation.

b. However, many well-established luxury brands (names you know well) espouse a strict non-negotiable price policy. Some customers may not like this; but for other clients, this can be a good thing. Some people actually prefer to pay the asking price, and that could be a benefit - these customers aren't put on the spot to try to negotiate on products that they don't have enough knowledge of or confidence in. It also means that everyone around the world who buys the same item from the same luxury retailer pays the same price. No savvy negotiators are afforded a better or discounted price because of their skills. This strict non-negotiation policy also enables the retailer to control the prices of their products across all their outlets. Furthermore, many luxury jewelers believe that fine jewelry is fine jewelry; and as such, it is priced accordingly. And there is no room...nor a need...for negotiations.

c. Additionally, there are customers who prefer to be treated like royalty while making such grand purchases. For them, the perceived value of their jewelry is enhanced the moment they savor the bubbly champagne, tasty treats, and exotic chocolates that are undoubtedly offered as a part of the superior service they receive during their luxurious shopping experience. For them, it's all about the refined ambiance and the cultured purchase process in as much as it is about the jewelry itself. As a part of becoming an elite client, it's about privilege, feeling upper-crust, and being treated like royalty. And the big luxury box stores look forward to this type of appreciative clientele walking through their impeccably cleaned doors.

2. In the end, does the price I pay determine the intrinsic value (or accepted industry value) of my piece?

A: No.

For example: if you find a wholesaler who's willing to sell to you, and s/he sells to you at a wholesale price (instead of at the higher retail price), congratulations! Your jewelry is likely to be "worth" more than you paid for it. And when it's independently appraised by a third party appraiser, you'll likely get a certificate of appraisal that supports this: your piece would be valued at considerably more than what you paid for it. In this case, you got a great buy from the wholesaler.

Conversely, you could pay an exorbitant retail price just for the privilege of shopping in a luxury store and carrying home a pretty box with a prestigious brand on the label. Your independent appraiser may estimate the monetary value of your new piece to be close to what you paid for it, but it could actually come out "worth" a little less than what you actually paid. In this case, it's good to remember that you had a great shopping experience and got to bring home a notable box that will impress your friends!

Another detail to note is the designer of your piece. If your jewelry has a well-respected hallmark on it, that may increase its value immensely. Sometimes designers are factored into the appraisals and sometimes they are not. It depends on who does the appraisal and how well-known the brand or the designer is.

As with any truly collectible art – and hand-crafted fine jewelry is most definitely a form of fine art – the brand name or celebrity designer on your piece can automatically increase the value of it. If your jewelry is signed by, or has the mark of, a famous jeweler, that insignia could add many thousands of dollars of instant value to your jewelry. After all, it comes from a proven and renown artiste. However, not every jeweler's name translates into value. As with any collectible art, make sure you understand the intangible and inherent value of the designer's name that is stamped into your piece.

** <u>Trick of the Trade</u>: There is a lot of margin in retail jewelry (meaning there's plenty of wiggle room to negotiate on the price). Because of this, we advise you to try to negotiate. Besides, believe it or not, most jewelers usually want to sell the item more than you want to buy it. Be advised, though, that there is a lot less room for negotiation on diamond pieces than there is on colored gemstones. Why? Industry-wide, diamond margins are very tight (because it's a strictly controlled market), and you will typically find that jewelers will remain firm on their diamond prices. They don't have as much room to play.

Just know that how ever you prefer to purchase your jewelry, there's no right or wrong in it. As long as you get your beautiful, prized piece for a price you think is fair and reasonable, then you've found yourself a valuable treasure. Congratulations!

Q: So what should I look for in a true "treasure?"

A: That's easy.

    a. Something you love.

    b. Something that has sentimental value to you.

    c. Something that has true intrinsic value in the quality of the materials used.

"Intrinsic value" is measured in SAVVY by what the jewelry industry esteems. What are the going rates of sapphires, diamonds, other exotic gems, and precious metals? What will continue to hold its value? What will have value in years to come when you want to pass your piece on to the next generation? What would a museum curator love to present in a showcase?

Keep in mind that SAVVY is all about making you a quick connoisseur of fine and exotic jewels. And in this luxurious world, it's all about natural gemstones, brilliant diamonds, and precious metals.

Anything else, according to SAVVY, is costume jewelry...and there is no slight meant towards these fashionable pieces. Ladies, we all have plenty of it. Our advice with costume or fashion jewelry: buy what you want, wear it often, and toss it when it goes out of style.

Our advice with fine jewels: buy what you love, wear it often, and know that quality jewelry is timeless and is always a perfect accompaniment for both casual and formal wear. Jeans or dresses, day or night, and every day of your life! There are no restrictions and no limitations. Buy quality and buy genuine...then you'll always be in vogue.

Now let SAVVY show you how to be a luxury jewel connoisseur and advise you of what to look for when purchasing fine jewelry and exotic gemstones...

2 – NATURAL & AU NATUREL

Quick Points

NATURAL – the *only* gemstone with true intrinsic value. It's what God created, not man. These jewels are the ones to collect.

LAB CREATED – may look pretty and be less expensive, but you get what you pay for. There is NO intrinsic value in a lab created stone. The only worth it may have is the cost of the resin used to create it (which is minimal). Toss these stones into the category of "fashion jewelry." And definitely don't pay any more for them than you would for costume jewelry.

ENHANCED – a little trickier. Some enhancements are standard and are wholly accepted by the international jewelry trade. Others are considered "cheating" and ruin the value of the stone.

Generally Accepted Enhancements

HEAT TREATMENT – almost all Sapphires are heat treated. So, too, are most Tanzanite. Generally speaking, many of the colored gemstones are almost always heat treated, and this treatment is used specifically to enhance the gem's color. It is such a common and ubiquitous practice that it's truly an industry standard. 99% of the sapphires you'll find have been heat treated. This is thought to add value to the gem, and it's accepted across the globe as a fair practice. Nevertheless, the 1% of fabulously colored sapphires that are natural in color, <u>not</u> heat treated, are immensely more valuable than their equivalent heat-treated cousins.

STABILIZING TURQUOISE – Approximately 97% of the turquoise on the market has been stabilized. It's about as commonplace as heat treatment is for sapphire. Stabilizing turquoise means that a <u>clear</u> resin has been added to the naturally soft, chalky stone to give it added hardness. This extra strength protects the soft stone. It also enables the turquoise to be drilled (without the gem disintegrating in the process) in order to be strung into a necklace or to be worked with while making jewelry. Stabilizing also shields and protects the stone from absorbing oils off the skin. Over time, oils from our skin could discolor the turquoise we love to wear; but when stabilized, the turquoise is protected from human oils and dirt, and therefore, it holds its natural color indefinitely.

   * Note: stabilized turquoise does *not* mean that it's dyed. Many turquoise products are stabilized with a <u>clear</u> resin. However, there are also manufacturers using colored resin, and that's technically considered *dying* the turquoise. Dyed turquoise *lowers* the intrinsic value of the stone. Be sure to ask your jeweler if the turquoise is natural, stabilized, and/or dyed. Natural and stabilized with a clear resin are good. Any dying treatments dramatically lower the worth of the stone.

RHODIUM PLATING – on metals. Rhodium plating enhances the shine of gold or silver and also protects the soft precious metals from scratching. It often adds a protective layer of reflective brilliance to the metal. Conversely, rhodium can also be used to darken metal to a blackish hue; and it's often employed for stylizing and designing pieces to give them an aged look.

Generally Rejected Treatments

The jewelry industry frowns upon these techniques.

DYES, COLORS, & TINTS – As with turquoise, no gemstone should be artificially dyed for better color. Heating a stone is different than dying it. Heating a stone encourages its natural colors to emerge (as if being baked in the Earth for another thousand years by Mother Nature). However, adding artificial dyes and color is *not* a natural process, and it also injects a man-made substance into the stone. This lowers the value of your gem.

SYNTHETIC STONES – Anything created in a lab by man (versus being created by Mother Earth) has no natural intrinsic value. Be aware that there are a multitude of lab created "rubies," "sapphires," "emeralds," and "amethysts" on the market. Also be aware that even though some of the more popular man-made stones have become prolific enough to warrant their own names, such as Cubic Zirconia, it does not mean that they have any true worth in the marketplace. Many stones, both natural and synthetic, garner names by which they are marketed. The names may be familiar and intriguing, such as Mystic Topaz, and the stones may be pretty, but synthetics have no true value.

When shopping, if you're not familiar with a stone, just ask detailed questions about its origin. You have every right to know what you're buying. You can also ask for it to be independently certified by the GIA (Gemological Institute of America), and that should ease all concerns.

AUTHOR'S NOTE:
Be aware that there are several 'independent labs' willing to certify gemstones with certificates of authenticity. The two labs we recommend are the GIA and the EGL (the European Gemological Laboratory). Both GIA and EGL certificates are the most

recognized and respected globally in the jewelry trade.

SYNTHETIC TOPICAL TREATMENTS – Meaning that a coating has been added to the stone to give it a 'magical' effect. Mystic Topaz is a great example of this. This "mystic" effect with its kaleidoscope of colors is created when a man-made titanic film is coated on top of a low-grade stone in order to give it a mystifying appearance. "Mystic Topaz" is a great marketing name for this lower-end stone. This enhanced 'topaz' (which may not actually be a topaz) is fun and colorful in costume jewelry. We recommend it for young girls, but not for those collecting fine jewelry. There are too many other genuine topaz (such as Imperial Topaz) that are truly incredible, rare, and highly valued jewels.

RECONSTITUTED STONES – This is a big No-No! Basically, this is a re-built stone. Low grade stones can be broken down or even ground down into a powder form. Then an epoxy resin is applied to the powder (usually with some dyes included as well) before it's re-compressed, shaped into specific forms or blocks, then baked as bricks until hardened before being cut into desired shapes for jewelry. This process can happen to many stones. Turquoise, because of its naturally soft, chalky texture, is one gem that can easily receive this treatment. Other porous stones can be manipulated similarly. Even emeralds – yes emeralds! – have been reconstituted and colored! Ask questions about the origin of your stone before purchasing.

** Trick of the Trade: one way to scan the stone, eye it, and judge quickly if it seems to be treated in some unacceptable way is to look at its color consistency. Is it too perfect? Is the blue of the turquoise so perfect that there are no blemishes (yet they are asking a low price for it)? Is your emerald's forest green color even (and the exact same intensity) throughout the entire stone? And, do all the emeralds in this particular collection have the same color tone, same clarity, and virtually same inclusions in approximately the same places within each of the stones? If so, then move on to the next jeweler. **No two gemstones (especially emeralds) are ever the same.** Their colors should vary, with different tonal qualities in different places within the stone itself, and their inclusions should be distinctive, unique, and in varying locations within each gem.

<u>Connoisseur's Quick Trick</u>: No two natural stones are ever the same. They all have characteristics and markings (even if subtle) that distinguish them from their siblings. If all the stones in a collection look exactly alike, especially if any inclusions look similar and are in virtually the same location within each stone, that's usually a sign of human tampering.

These are just some of the more common stone treatments found in the industry; however, there are other forms of human enhancements, both acceptable and unacceptable. If ever in doubt, check with your trusted jeweler and/or do some online research before purchasing anything you question.

** Note: ask for your gem to be certified by an independent third party lab (GIA or EGL) before you buy it. This will clarify quickly any concerns you may have about the stone's origin, value, or suspected enhancements.

FOR DIAMONDS – <u>IRRADIATION</u> is a common treatment. This means that the jewels have been radiated (and then annealed) to produce the desired color you see. Because the diamond market is so tightly controlled, irradiation doesn't necessarily affect the worth of the diamond. However, you need to know that an irradiated diamond is not valued anywhere near the likes of a natural fancy colored diamond, especially fancy diamonds with their origins from the Argyle mine of Australia. When diamond colors are natural, they are measured in the "fancy" ranges; and the intrinsic values of the highest quality fancy diamonds jump up exponentially into the tens…and even hundreds…of thousands of dollars per carat range.

<u>Connoisseur's Quick Trick</u>: Natural, fancy colored diamonds are typically more pastel in comparison to their irradiated cousins, yet they often glow with a deeper, more constant and resilient brilliance from the inside out. Although fancy yellows and pinks can be extremely vibrant, an <u>irradiated</u> stone has a truly unnatural electric neon coloring that almost looks painted, even "thick." Again, if the color tone of your gem is virtually the same as all of the other diamonds in the collection, and if none of the stones have any uniqueness in their hues or individual personality, that's a give-away that they are likely treated. Teal blues (meaning there is a greenish cast overlaying the base blue color), forest greens, and banana yellows tend to be the most popular colors for irradiated diamonds. When these radiated stones are further annealed (given a specific type of heat treatment), the greens and blues turn to shades of orange, pink, and brown.

** Note: Nothing beats a 100% natural gem, especially if it's certified. It will always retain its intrinsic value and will carry a higher worth than any treated stone.

3 – PHENOMENAL

Phenomena Gemstones

Synthetic phenomena gemstones are also created in labs, and the same rules apply as above: if the phenomenon is too perfect, too clean, too visible at all angles and in all lighting situations, it's likely not natural. Lindy star sapphires are great examples of phenomena stones that are too perfect to be real.

Types of Natural Phenomena in Gemstones

ADULARESCENCE – a "cloudy" appearance in an otherwise transparent or semi-transparent stone. The resulting diffused light gives it appealing character and a highly mobile sheen.
Gem praised for this trait:
Moonstone
(blue is the most prized color with peach moonstones rising in popularity)

ASTERISM – the "star" effect, usually seen as a 4- or 6-pointed star. Caused by needle-like inclusions within the stone. Best seen when the stone is cut en cabochon.
Gems commonly known to display stars:
Sapphires, Rubies, Rose Quartz

CHATOYANCY – a "cat's eye" caused naturally by threadlike inclusions in the stone.

Gems known to display cat's eyes:

> Chrysoberyl, Alexandrite, Quartz (such as Tiger's Eye and Hawk's Eye), Tourmaline

COLOR CHANGE – the color of the stone changes in different lighting situations, such as when going from daylight to candlelight. Gems such as the Alexandrite show purplish red in incandescent lighting and green in natural daylight. The color shift of many gems usually moves from the green/blue range to the red/purple range. For example, it is said that Alexandrite is "emerald by day and ruby by night."

Gems that display significant color change:

> Alexandrite, Color-Change Garnets, Color-Change Sapphires

IRIDESCENCE – when the surface of the stone appears to have multiple colors simultaneously. It's a widespread phenomenon among gemstones.

Gems that usually display beautiful iridescence:

> Pearls, Mother of Pearl, Labradorite, Fire Agate, Ammolite, Fine Opal

4 – DETERMINING VALUE

Determining Value

Q: How is a gemstone valued?

A: By its intrinsic value, quality, rarity/scarcity, and market demand.

Since market demand can be influenced by a variety of external and man-made factors, we'll focus here on the natural factors: quality (as measured by the "four C's") and geologic rarity/scarcity.

Rarity vs Scarcity:

The laws of economics tell us that when something is scarce (hard to find) and that there is also a demand for it, its price inevitably rises. That makes sense. When more people are vying for something hard to find, it becomes more 'valuable.'

The same applies to the world of gemstones, but sometimes at an even more rapid and escalated pace.

As we define here in SAVVY, rarity is different than scarcity. "Scarcity" can be thought of as a shortage…whereas "rarity" can be used to describe something that is highly uncommon, infrequent or even curiously unique.

CURRENTLY SCARCE GEMS:

White Sapphire, Pink Sapphire, Pink Tourmaline, true "Pool-Water Blue" Aquamarine, Cobalt Blue Tanzanite, Tsavorite Garnet (over 2 carats in size), Demantoid Garnet, Mandarin Garnet (highly intense tangerine orange sun-color), Rubellite Tourmaline, Sleeping Beauty Turquoise (from the Sleeping Beauty mine in Arizona), and Coral.

These stones can still be acquired, it just takes more effort to search for them, to find the right quality, and to find the ideal cut.

Scarce gemstones move into the "Rare" category when they're almost mined out and/or are totally off the market. When this happens, their values increase exponentially…and it can happen overnight! It's often so dramatic when this occurs that some professionals in the industry refer to these stones as "becoming extinct."

CURRENTLY RARE GEMS:

Sardinian Coral, Russian Alexandrite, Russian Demantoid Garnet, Tanzanian Pink Spinel, Pool Water Blue Copper Bearing Tourmaline, Sweet Home Mine Rhodochrosite, Burmese Ruby, and Burmese Imperial Jade.

If you'll notice, the gems named above aren't just general classifications of gemstones (such as "sapphire" or "garnet"), but they're extremely specific – qualified by prized color and/or origin. A stone's origin, especially when the mine closes or is no longer accessible, plays a critical factor in the rarity, and thus the value, of the stone. For example, sapphires can be obtained from many locations around the world: in Asia, in Africa, and even in the

United States (Montana). But the most valuable blue sapphire in the world today cannot be found anywhere. The incredible Kashmir Sapphire is an extraordinary museum-quality jewel that many jewelry professionals would call "extinct." Hands down, it's nowhere to be found. The only ones known today are in collections.

CURRENTLY <u>EXTINCT</u> GEMS:
Kashmir Blue Sapphire (from Kashmir, India) and
Paraiba Tourmaline (out of Paraiba, Brazil)

Some Rare and Scarce Gems you may want to add to your collection before they become "extinct" are:

Tanzanian Pink Spinel
Mandarin Garnet
Colorado Rhodochrosite (from Sweet Home Mine)
Blocks A & B Tanzanite (deepest cobalt blue color)
Tsavorite Garnet (over 2 carats)
Russian Demantoid Garnet
African Chrome Tourmaline
Muzo Mine Emerald (from Columbia)
Pink Diamond (from the Argyle mine in Australia)
Sleeping Beauty Turquoise (from the Sleeping Beauty mine in Arizona)

Some of the mines associated with a few of the stones above are permanently closed or soon will be.

Many of these scarce and rare gemstones come exclusively from one mine in only one location in the world. That's called a "one-source gem." When that sole location dries up, that often indicates the end of that particular gemstone.

Collectors beware...and jewelry lovers, be aware.

5 – THE 4 C'S

Of course, when purchasing gems, you'll want the highest quality you can find. How do you know the best quality? By following the standard of the "4 C's..."

The "4 C's" for Colored Stones

Many people actually refer to it as the "5 C's." We'll explain the fifth C when we get to it. However, for <u>colored</u> gemstones, the first, and most critical, 4 C's are:

COLOR – ideal color is THE MOST IMPORTANT factor in choosing a <u>colored</u> gemstone. (Consistency, intensity, and depth of color throughout the entire stone is of equal vital importance).

CLARITY – meaning lack of inclusions. There are no inherent flaws in the stone that are visible to the eye. Being 'clean' is extremely important...but it remains secondary behind color quality for colored gemstones. (Some stones, like garnets, should be perfectly clean; and others, like emeralds, are expected to have some inclusions). Red stones, by their nature, are the most prone to having inclusions – so when you see a beautifully clean rubellite tourmaline or a perfect ruby, know that's a heck of a gem. Type III gemstones, such as emerald and red tourmaline, are expected to have inclusions visible to the naked eye. This is not considered a flaw, rather more of a unique characteristic to that particular gem. In fact, these 'imperfections' are thought to give each stone its own unique personality. These nuances can be complimentary and endearing. Nevertheless, the cleaner (inclusion-free) a Type III gem is, the better…and the finer it's considered to be.

CUT (and shape) – mastery is needed here. Color gemstones can be cut into more varieties of shapes than diamonds can be (because of the different internal mineral structures within colored stones). However, the gem's cut, as with diamonds, is critical: the stone's internal characteristics, natural axis, chemical lattice, growth patterns, final size, reflection of color, and ideal proportions for the desired shape all must be adhered to. A pretty gem with a bad cut can render the stone very low in value. Conversely, a perfectly colored stone cut ideally to enhance the play of light (and color) through the stone can add immense worth to the jewel. This is why stone cutting mastery takes years to achieve, and only the most talented lapidaries (gemstone cutters) are employed when dealing with exotic, high-end jewels.

CARAT (weight) – how colored gems and diamonds are weighed. A carat can be broken down into 100 points (like a dollar is broken down into 100 cents). The carat's origin goes back to ancient days when dual scales were used to weigh gems. On one side of the scale would sit the gemstone; and on the other side, carob beans would be placed as a counter measure until the accurate weight of the stone could be assessed. Naturally, carob beans fluctuate in size and weight; and it wasn't until a century ago that the actual weight of a carob was finally standardized – one carob bean was decreed to equal to 0.200 grams. The "carat" was then adopted as the official standard of measurement for gemstones by the US in 1913 and by Britain in 1914. By the 1930's, most of the international countries involved in the gemstone trade had adopted the carat as their official measurement for gemstone weights.

CERTIFICATION – is the "Fifth C," and it is typically used for diamond grading. It's an official gemological lab certification of your gem, listing its attributes and certifying its authenticity. You certainly can get lab certifications for colored gemstones as well, especially on the more exotic, rare, and valuable ones. In fact, we advise you to ask for a certification if you're making a large purchase. It helps to ease your mind when you certify your gem (and the certificate confirms that you're actually buying a fabulous jewel). It will also certify the origin of your colored stone! The cert is also critical for insurance purposes. Most insurance companies will ask for a copy of your cert for identification purposes. Again, we recommend GIA or EGL lab certifications.

Likewise, certifying a diamond upon purchase means that you'll get affirmation of your diamond's qualities and characteristics.

Certifications do not always give estimated monetary value of your gems. If you wish for monetary estimates, you may also need to get an appraisal.

** A Statement on Diamonds **

Diamonds naturally adhere to the rule of the 5 C's, but the order of priority for which "C" is most important differs from that of colored gems. With diamonds, **Carat** weight and **Cut** receive the highest priorities. After that, color and clarity come into play.

Diamonds are their own category of jewels for many reasons, and they are rated differently than color gemstones. Their *size* and *brilliance* capture attention, and it's for those reasons that diamonds are graded the way they are. That's why **carat weight** and **cut** are the two most important traits of a diamond solitaire. (Whereas with colored gemstones, it's the...well, *color*...that catches the eye and becomes the primary way to judge a quality color gem).

When buying a diamond solitaire, feel free to ask for its cert. That is the "5th C" after all. It will confirm for you what the valuable attributes of the jewel are: the carat weight, the cut, the proportions of the cut, the color, and the clarity. Whether you can see the subtle differences in a brilliant diamond with the naked eye or not, the certification will help you to insure your gem; and it will definitely come in handy if you ever go to re-sell it in the future.

AUTHOR'S NOTE:
Beware of small sparkles. Some manufacturers cut corners by layering their jewelry with diamond chips. Relatively speaking, these chips have little to no value although they can deceive the eye and look shiny. In luxury goods, you do <u>not</u> want diamond chips.

Diamond melee is better. What is melee? These are small brilliant-cut *whole* diamonds that are usually used as accent stones in smaller, more delicate areas of jewelry, such as along the basket and shaft of a ring. Melee do retain value because they are individual, whole, faceted diamonds...as opposed to chips, which are just diamond pieces adhered to the surface of a base metal.

Summary:
The 4 (or 5) C's measure the gemstone's quality from an unbiased, scientific quantitative and qualitative (subjective) perspective. A stone's geologic rarity and scarcity also add to its intrinsic value. If you find a gem that scores high with all the C's and also has high market demand, then you will have a jewel that is HIGHLY VALUABLE...especially the rarer it becomes!

6 – WHAT TO BUY

What To Buy?

Now that you know what you're looking for regarding quality, rarity, phenomena, and authenticity, where do you start?

How about with something you like, have always wanted, or when its beauty simply compels you?

If you're considering purchasing jewelry to celebrate a special occasion, at the back of this book on p. 91, there are appendices listing birthstones and anniversary commemorative gems to help you honor momentous dates.

If you're buying for the fun of it, we also suggest some remarkable gems for you to consider. These gemstones are categorized below based on the following classifications: Precious & Semi-Precious (following older industry categories), and "Brilliant," "Rule Breakers," and "Fan Favorites" (SAVVY's own unique classifications).

Gems to Consider

PRECIOUS

Well established and well known:
Sapphires, Rubies, Emeralds
(also includes Alexandrite & Padparadscha)

It's a CORUNDUM Conundrum!

What does that mean? Simply put, rubies and sapphires are the same type of stone. They come from the same family of rock – they're both Corundum. So you can think of rubies as red sapphires if you wish. You'd be correct. Sapphires, by the way, come in a variety of colors (not just blue). Some of the more popular sapphire hues are yellow, pink, white, purple, and padparadscha (a perfect blend of pink and orange, giving the stone a vibrant peachy glow). Sapphires even display the phenomena of color change and asterism.

So when choosing your Corundum, go for the color and the stone that most intrigues you. Make sure it's the highest quality stone you can afford (following the 4 C's), and you'll have a treasure. You can't go wrong with a Corundum.

If you want rarity and higher worth, search for natural colors (not heat treated). Pink, perfect blue (Kashmir blue or Ceylon blue), and padparadscha are prized sapphire colors. Regarding rubies, any quality stone with a Burmese origin will grow immensely in value. Moreover, the Burmese rubies characteristically have a neon pink overtone that sets them apart from rubies out of Africa and other areas of the world, which are typically more brick or blood red in their base colors. That pink neon glow gives Burmese rubies their prized status.

EMERALDS – they were Cleopatra's favorite, and they remain royalty in the gemstone world even today. Emeralds, however, are <u>not</u> corundum, rather they belong to the Beryl family of stones; but they are the variety of Beryl that is considered "precious" by old-world industry standards.

Egyptian emeralds are all but gone; but it's the Muzo Mine in Columbia, South America, that in modern times is generally regarded as producing the best emeralds. Muzo Mine stones have a dark, rich, Amazonian jungle green undertone, highlighted by lime (neon) green flashes, accents, and overtones. When clean from inclusions, they look as if they could glow in the dark! Broadly speaking, any genuine emerald you see that has a forest green base color with neon highlights will likely come from Columbia, South America. It may not come from the Muzo Mine, but Columbian emeralds are generally regarded as world class gems because of their color-play. Look for their characteristic neon lime green glow.

Also, expect that your emerald will have inclusions. In fact, it *should* have inclusions. The clusters of imperfections in emeralds are affectionately regarded to as the "garden" (or "le jardin") by the jewelry industry. These unique "gardens" give each emerald their own personality and distinguishing characteristics. However, the finest of emeralds will have very few visible flaws, and the "garden" should be miniscule…but it should be in there somewhere.

** <u>Trick of the Trade</u>: That's a great way to test whether you're looking at a genuine emerald or at a synthetic (or at a manipulated, enhanced stone): the garden should be visible (even if minimal), and it should be unique within the stone, meaning that its size, shape and location are different than in other emeralds. Each emerald should stand alongside all of its siblings and proudly showcase its unique play of light, tonal qualities, and personality, causing it to be distinctly different than all the other emeralds.

ALEXANDRITE – Alexandrite hail from the Chrysoberyl family of stones, and Russian Alex's are regarded as the best. Alexandrite is extremely rare, and it has a double refractive index. What does that mean? In layman's terms, it means that Alexandrite shines brilliantly. But what makes Alexandrite stand out and be so unique among other gemstones is that it should also exhibit a high degree of color change (usually above 85-90% color change indicates a good stone). An Alex's color will morph between red and green depending upon the lighting.

*Note: these gems typically come in small sizes. A standard faceted Alex might be less than 1 carat. If you come across a beautiful Alex with nice color change that is larger than 1½ carats, grab it!

BRILLIANT

What makes a stone brilliant? Its shine. You know it when you see it. It seems to glow from within (because it's reflecting and refracting light, playing with the color spectrum, and oftentimes causing a prismatic effect that separates white light into its spectral colors). The dazzling display of light, the flashing color array, its unstoppable shine and high luster all combine to make a stone scintillatingly brilliant.

Some gems are singularly refractive, and others have "double refractive indices." Without getting too technical, a "double refractive index" slows the speed of light down when it enters the gemstone, and it slows the white light down at two different velocities. These light waves then bounce through the stone at two different speeds (thus double refraction) and cause the light to be reflected back out of the gem at multiple angles and at different rates, thus giving the stone a more brilliant appearance.

Many of the gems in our "Brilliant" category are listed because they are visibly brilliant, and their brilliance is often due to a "double refractive index" inherent in the stone.

Brilliant Stones to consider adding to your collection are:

ZIRCON – especially the incredible teal blue zircon from Cambodia. It's naturally doubly refractive, and light dances spectacularly through it.

** Note: Zircon is a <u>natural gemstone</u> with a double refractive index. It's dazzling and beautiful and comes in many colors, such as white, cognac, blue, and red. Do NOT confuse it with Cubic Zirconia, a synthetic diamond-like crystal. Cubic Zirconia is costume jewelry at best. <u>Natural Zircon stones are truly fine gems!</u>

DEMANTOID GARNET – derives its name "Demantoid" from the German word for "diamond-like" because of its brilliance. High quality demantoid garnets are lime and pastel green, and they are so blinding one would think they could glow in the dark!

SPHENE – is a rare collector's gem with an incredibly high dispersion and refractive index. It displays stunning brilliance, but it also has an added optical phenomena called "fire," which is where the light is broken down into its spectral colors, just as in a prism. The result is a fabulous display of rich gem hues creating a dazzling rainbow that appears to radiate effortlessly from the stone. It is a beautiful, fabulous, and 100% natural (<u>not</u> heat treated) gem! Its base color may be yellowish golden, green or honey brown, but every primary color dances vibrantly out of it.

DIAMONDS – remember that <u>carat</u> weight and <u>cut</u> are the most important attributes with faceted diamonds. A proper cut on a diamond will add to its incredible natural brilliance. This amazing sparkle is often referred to as "scintillation." When a luxurious diamond scintillates, your eye is actually detecting the infinite sparks of color from a spectacular light-play as the white light passes through the diamond's many facets and is broken up into its spectral colors, many of which are emitted rapidly out of the gem as blue, red, orange, and yellow flashes.

Additionally, natural "fancy" stone colors can add great value to diamonds. However, if you don't want a fancy colored diamond, remember that you're actually looking for NO color in your diamond. The less color, or the most colorless, a diamond is, the better. You don't want a white diamond (although many people refer to a colorless diamond as "white," but that's a misnomer) because white insinuates some hint of color. You want your diamond to be as colorless as possible. Also, the less inclusions it has (the cleaner it is), the better.

D-E-F grade diamonds are the most colorless. These are the highest colorless grades available, and they are difficult to find. This quality of diamond is not typically shown on retail showroom floors, but you can ask a high-end retailer to possibly pull one from the vault for you.

The color grade works its way down the alphabet. D color(less) is the best, and it's better than E. E is better than F. Yet D, E, and F diamonds are grouped as the best on the market and are very hard to find. In fact, many jewelers won't even carry them in stock.

Many luxury retailers stay with the G color diamonds. They are brilliant, near colorless, and are still considered high quality. So if someone tells you they have a G-colored diamond, it is definitely worth looking at.

Diamond clarity (meaning how many inclusions it has) starts at "Flawless" and works its way down the scale to several grades of "Included." Generally speaking, with the exception of Flawless, VVS is the cleanest diamond available on the market. VVS means "very very slightly" included (and that inclusion is only seen under heavy scrutiny while viewed under the magnification of a microscope). VVS is an extremely nice diamond. The next step down from VVS is VS, "very slightly" included. It, too, has extremely nice clarity; and oftentimes, VVS and VS diamonds are used interchangeably in mountings, especially when they're being used as accent stones.

Many jewelers carry diamonds in the SI-1 and SI-2 ranges, which means "slightly included." This is the level where inclusions start to become visible to the naked eye...and definitely visible when viewed through a loupe or under magnification. You can often tell SI diamonds (especially when placed next to VVS & VS jewels) because the SI diamonds start to look a little "cloudy." When diamonds lose their clarity, they also begin to lose their brilliance.

There is a full diamond grading scale on pg. 82 at the back of this guide for further clarification.

Generally speaking, though, if you're searching for luxury goods, you should be able to find diamonds that are VS clarity with G color or better. If someone is selling you SI-2, H color diamonds (or worse), you're not in the fine goods market anymore.

Natural fancy colored diamonds add value (and cost) to your diamond; but clarity still plays a very important role in the overall worth of your gem.

SEMI-PRECIOUS

Don't let the name fool ya! In fact, we at SAVVY are not fans of this categorization; however, it is an older standard classification within the jewelry industry, and because of that, we'll use it here, too.

"Semi-Precious" was once a title used to refer to colored gems that weren't valued as highly as the tried-and-true "precious" gems like sapphires, rubies, and emeralds – the "Big Three." Because of this strict, and oftentimes looked down upon, 'semi-precious' classification, every other colored gem that landed in a jewelry store ended up classified as 'semi-precious.' Such stones include tourmaline, amethyst, blue topaz, peridot, garnet, citrine, iolite, aquamarine, amber, coral and virtually any other gemstone that's not a diamond or one of the original "Big Three."

However, truth be known – and we're proud to report – that many of these so-called "semi-precious" gems have risen quietly through the ranks. In fact, countless international luxury jewelry companies (you know their names) now prominently display "semi-precious" stones as their center signature gems in their most prized collections. We can't tell you how many of the highest-end retailers use semi-precious materials in their main showcases. In fact, we were surprised. When amethyst, aquamarine, and citrine (along with mother-of-pearl and other materials) are the focus of designer jewelry collections, that tells us a couple of things: 1. 'Semi-precious' has moved into prominence; 2. The current economy dictates that less costly center stones are more economically viable for both the retailer and its customers; and 3. Jewelry lovers and collectors are searching for more variety…and color…in their jewelry collections.

So don't let the term 'semi-precious' throw you at all. In fact, in our next section, we'll list for you all the 'semi-precious' gems that have broken the rules and are now in such great demand that they oftentimes garner more money per carat than "the Big Three" precious stones. They are also so rare that collectors will pay prices in the tens of thousands of dollars *per carat* just to have one.

Currently some of the most common 'semi-precious' stones that you'll find in the retail markets today are:

TOURMALINE – of all colors. Pink Tourmaline is one of the most demanded hues. Green tourmaline and watermelon tourmaline are also popular. Red tourmaline, also known as "Rubellite," is more rare and valuable, especially if it's clean and has no inclusions. Tourmaline is found in every color of the rainbow. Some reports state that tourmaline has been discovered in over 30,000 hues. It's also typically a highly included stone, but you want it to be as inclusion-free as possible. Transparent is your goal. By the way, Tourmaline is the official national gemstone of the United States.

AMETHYST – a member of the Quartz family. Yes, it's purple quartz. Some of your fine retailers choose a lovely mid-tone lavender shade for their showcase pieces; however, in the industry and by collector's standards, deep royal purple is the most prized color. Siberian (Russian) amethyst is the most valuable; and it's so velvety rich in royal purple that it often emits blue and red flashes. If you can't get a Russian amethyst, look for a Uruguayan. Uruguayan amethyst is almost as dark as Siberian, and it is also highly prized.

** Note: buyers beware – dark royal purple amethyst is one of the most synthetically replicated gemstones. It's a favorite for labs who create synthetics and then slide them into the marketplace as genuine. Find a trusted jeweler, and even ask for a GIA cert if you want proof your amethyst is genuine.

CITRINE – the golden variety of amethyst. Why? Because citrine is created by heating amethyst. Citrine's coloring is well monitored. As long as the golden hues exhibit rich coloring within gold or sunset yellow colors (such as with the highly prized Madeira Citrine, which has autumnal sunset orange overtones to it, adding richness to the base golden color), then it is classified as a citrine. There is a separate category of stones that are "yellow" quartz, but that is truly a yellow quartz (not a heated amethyst). Yellow quartz is usually a much more stereotypical lemon yellow and pale in comparison to a true citrine.

** Note: Ametrine is a very popular stone. It's a bi-colored gem that combines the purple of amethyst with the gold of citrine. Thus the combination name, "ametrine." Look for an ametrine with rich, distinctive color tones and a clean color division that is delineated midway through the stone.

AUTHOR'S NOTE:
There is a stone now in the marketplace called "Prasiolite." It is a green amethyst, and most prasiolite are created by heat treating amethyst. As with citrine, which is also a heated amethyst, "prasiolite" receives its own industry name. When a heated amethyst yields a green stone instead of the rich gold of a citrine, it's called Prasiolite. By the FTC guidelines, a heated amethyst that results in a green stone must be called "prasiolite," not green quartz. That's to keep it distinguished from naturally occurring green quartz, which does form throughout the world (in places such as Brazil, Poland, and Canada). But a heat-treated amethyst that results in a green stone (instead of golden yellow 'citrine') is called a "prasiolite."

BERYL – calling this gem by the stone's family name is rather unglamorous. But if you call it "golden beryl," "red beryl" (rare and valuable), "morganite" (the pink variety of beryl), or even "aquamarine" (the blue-green variety), now we're talking gems! Because of the values that some red beryl and certain aquamarine garner, these gemstones are priced sometimes as high as precious gemstones, if not more so.

** Note: Aquamarine has a favored, prized coloring. It is the perfect "swimming pool blue" color, and the intensity should be consistent throughout the entire stone. This consistent coloring gives the gem's tone depth and a refreshing quality. The highest prized aquamarine stones come from the Santa Maria mine in Brazil. If you hear it's a Santa Maria aqua, take a look at it (but then scrutinize it according to the 4C standards. And make sure you're truly getting the ideal "swimming pool blue" color).

*** Note: the prized color of aquamarine less than a century ago — in the mid-1900's — was a "seafoam green" color. "Seafoam green" is a pastel green that is reminiscent of shallow salt water. This shade was popular until the Santa Maria mine opened and its exquisite saturated "swimming pool" blues were discovered.

AUTHOR'S NOTE:
The beryl family of stones is as equally vibrant and rich as others. Keep in mind that the deep green variety of beryl is more commonly referred to as "emerald." So when you see aquamarine or morganite, know that these are the blue-green and pink cousins, respectively, of emerald. As far as red beryl goes, it has no known commercial name other than the mundane "red beryl." But it could be considered an extremely rare "red emerald." How about that?! And considering that red is one of the hardest colors for Mother Earth to create in minerals, a "red beryl" is a rarity...and, yes, it is an expensive and extremely valuable exotic gemstone.

So to sum up, it is this author's opinion that 'semi-precious' is a gross misnomer. For example, beryl stones can slide into the "precious" category (with emeralds) or stay at the top of the 'semi-precious' charts (with aquamarine and morganite). Or it can become priceless and invaluable (with "red beryl"). Garnets, like beryl, can also slide toward extremely high-end (and rare), toppling the semi-precious charts and costing far more per carat than any of "the Big Three" original precious stones.

Other semi-precious gems are much more common, such as quartz. And quartz is...well...quartz, although it is a beautiful stone that comes in a rainbow of colors.

It really is the popularity of color gemstones, along with their rarity, that adds value to them. And "semi-precious" is a term that in modern times is being used less and less and is generally considered mostly out-of-date...and rightly so!

Now that you see how stones can be traditionally classified...and how those classifications may not necessarily represent the true worth of the gems...let us introduce you to a few of the better known rule breakers.

RULE BREAKERS

The Rule Breakers listed here are gems that have such high demand that they have become incredibly valuable – regardless of how they may have originally been classified in traditional 'precious' & 'semi-precious' jewelry categories.

** AUTHOR'S NOTE & DISCLAIMER:
We are not licensed to, nor do we assume to, give you financial advice regarding investments or gemstone purchases. The statements made in SAVVY are based on gemstone history and from watching the value of scarce gems continue to rise over the years...especially as they become more and more rare. The value the jewelry industry places on these jewels continues to increase as the availability of these stones continues to decrease. It's simply supply and demand for a gem that is no longer easily obtained. There are many factors for this such as: the mine is mined out, the mine is only accessible for a couple of months per year, or government-imposed economic sanctions against a country artificially cut off the flow of natural minerals out of that country (Burma comes to mind). Based on a variety of industry factors, coupled with geologic rarity, we recommend the following Rule Breaker gems for aficionados and collectors to add to their collections. **However, this is NOT investment advice, nor is it intended to be.** This is fun for jewelry and gemstone lovers and connoisseurs looking to expand their repertoires.

If you can find any of these Rule Breakers in high quality, they're definitely worth adding to your colorful collection:

Rule Breaker Gems

Gemstone	Special Color/Trait	Other
Paraiba Tourmaline	Ideal Color: Aged Copper Patina (that rich green-blue patina), the deeper, the better Also Valuable: Neon Swimming Pool Blue	Origin = Brazil (First brought to market in 1989)
Copper Bearing Tourmaline	Neon Swimming Pool Blue, like Paraiba	Origin = Nigeria & Mozambique, Africa Paraiba's cousin. High concentration of gold elements in the stone. (First brought to market in 2005)
Copper Bearing Tourmaline	Pink	Origin = Africa
Chrome Tourmaline	Deepest, darkest green	Origin = Africa Look for stones 2.0 carats or larger. Chrome tourmaline differs from green tourmaline in that it truly has traces of chromium in the gem. With a trained eye, you can actually see the deeper, darker depth of the green tones in chrome tourmaline

Popsicle Tourmaline	Dark Blue that appears greenish at certain angles	Origin = Brazil, Anywhere
Indicolite Tourmaline	Solidly Darkest Blue	Origin = Anywhere
Tsavorite Garnet	Dark Amazonian Jungle Green	Origin = Tsavo Park, Kenya Look for a stone larger than 2.0 carats. (First brought to market in the 1970's)
Mandarin Garnet	Electric Tangerine Orange	Origin = Namibia & Nigeria, Africa The fastest appreciating gemstone in modern history. (First brought to market in 1993)
Imperial Topaz	Deep honey gold with peach and red accents	Origin = Ouro Prêto, Brazil
Pink Spinel	Electric Hot Pink	Origin = Tanzania, Africa Spinel is never heated or treated in any way. It's one of the few gemstones truly unaffected by man. Its colors are vibrant and au naturel!

Spinel	Any Color	This is one of Earth's rarest and most beautiful natural gems. Spinel is not heated or treated in any way – ever! Its hardness is almost equal to that of corundum (sapphire & ruby), but it's much more rare than corundum!
Tanzanite	Cobalt Blue with red flashes	Origin = Tanzania, Africa Initially mined from Blocks A & B, which are known to produce the best color saturation and quality of Tanzanite. (First brought to market in 1967 as a substitute for Kashmir Sapphire)
Rhodochrosite	Hot Glowing Electric Pink	Origin = Sweet Home Mine, Colorado Rare in this vibrant pink hue and even more rare as a faceted gemstone (because it's difficult to cut and shape this naturally soft stone)

There are countless gems that could make our list of "Rule Breakers," but the above chart contains the hottest exotic gemstones on the market today.

If you're a purist and are still building your collection, some more traditional "Fan Favorites" are sure to offer you a diversified, unique, and beautiful jewelry collection.

FAN FAVORITES

Gemstone	What to Look For
Amber	Prized Origins: Baltic (Poland) and Russia Similar quality can be found throughout central northern Europe. Golden rich yellow, like the gold of autumn. Look for an ancient, encapsulated insect within your stone. That's highly prized!
Coral	Variety of Colors: Red, Pink, Black Most Prized: Sardinian (fire-engine red) and Mediterranean coral. Other Popular Colors: Angel Skin (pastel pink), Salmon (rich pink), Ox-Blood Coral (deep rich blood red, usually used in Native American jewelry), and Black. Black Coral is a protected species, and it is regulated and is used sparingly. Look for unique characteristics within the black for growth patterns, "fire" (flashes of red), and "mutations" (some natural sandy brown coloring still coating the polished black). Black coral is not as easily found as red and pink.
Jade	Prized Origin: Burma Prized Color: Emerald Green (known as "Imperial Jade") Type Desired: Jadeite Jade Other Popular Color: Lavender * Lesser valued Jade: serpentine, Transvaal, Pakistani, and imitation Jade ** Beware of "impregnated" stones

Lapis Lazuli	Prized Origin: Afghanistan Natural Gold Pyrite flecks in stone are highly prized. Look for the gold.
Moonstone	Fun Phenomena Stone Prized Color: Blue (Peach Moonstone is also popular)
Quartz (includes Amethyst, Citrine, Ametrine, and Prasiolite)	Have Fun! Most Popular Varieties: Amethyst and Citrine Other popular varieties: Rose Quartz, Smoky Quartz, Yellow Quartz, Dendritic Quartz, and Tiger's Eye
Topaz	Prized Origin: Brazil Prized Color: Imperial Topaz Imperial Topaz is honey colored with red tones accenting the stone (especially at the edges), giving it a peachy glow. Other Popular Colors: Blue and White Popular Blue Tones: Swiss Blue (bright, electric), London Blue (dark blue), and Sky Blue A great gem for everyday wear. Topaz is a vibrant gem in any collection.
Turquoise	Prized Origin: Persia Most prized color: "Sleeping Beauty Blue" or "Robin Egg Blue." Sometimes seen with copper flecks in stone. Currently Popular: Arizona Turquoise (aka. "Mojave Turquoise") Arizona stones come in various colors: Blue, Green, Purple - usually showing some of the matrix (black streaks) and other minerals (such as copper) that are

	embedded with the turquoise in its host geologic formations. Natural Turquoise is best. Stabilized is OK, but NOT dyed. Popular and Hard to Find: Genuine Sleeping Beauty turquoise from the original Sleeping Beauty mine (in Globe, AZ). It's the stone that gave "Sleeping Beauty Blue" its color name.

Aside from these stones, most any mineral can be used for decoration and jewelry, and they often are. Larimar, aventurine, malachite, obsidian, jet, howlite, sodalite and other lesser known and exotics are regularly used.

Some of the more favored gems throughout history have survived the test of time due to their ageless beauty, bountiful supply, and enduring popularity. Such stones are what we consider to be "time honored."

TIME HONORED GEMS

Gemstone	What to Look For
Amethyst	Prized Origin: Siberia (Russia) Next Best Origin: Uruguay Prized Color: richest, velvety **deep royal purple** with flashes of blue and red. When you imagine "royal purple" velvet, the kind kings wear in paintings, you are envisioning the color of a perfect amethyst. The best colors are found in gems from Siberia and Uruguay. You will find amethyst offered in all shades

	of purple, ranging from pastel to lavender to almost a soft pink. Generally speaking, the darker the stone, the better. However, if you love the look of a piece of jewelry with a subtle shade of lavender amethyst, enjoy it. More often than not, you'll find the lighter shades being offered in most retail stores. In the Victorian era, the dainty pastel lavender shade called "rose de France" was a very popular color of amethyst. Overall, it's much harder to find a genuine royal purple amethyst…and when you do find it, grab it! ** Beware of synthetic amethyst, especially Russian made synthetics. They're beautiful, but they have *zero* intrinsic value.
Emerald	Prized Origin: Columbia, South America (Muzo Mine preferred) Rich **forest green** color with neon green overtones or flashes. Minimal Inclusions (but it should have some), affectionately called the "garden." ** Beware of reconstituted or filled stones

Garnet	A gem with its roots in ancient times. Many people think of garnets as brick red with a brownish tint. Those typically are your lower-end stones. Garnets naturally come in a rainbow of colors. And like Spinel, they are not heated or treated by humans in any way. (The only exception is the Demantoid Garnet. It is sometimes mildly heated to enhance its vibrance). Most popular (non-brick red) Garnets: Tsavorite (vibrant Amazonian **green**), Ant Hill Garnet (cabernet **red**), Spessartite – including Mandarins (rich deep orange with cognac-colored undertones. Mandarins have elevated levels of manganese which give them their vibrant neon **tangerine** hues), Demantoid (pastel and lime green), Green Grossular (rich crayon green), Rhodolite (perfect lipstick red), and Color Change Garnet. * Russian Demantoid Garnet is rarer than Alexandrite and can be more costly than Diamond! It is truly a rare and valued gem. ** Be sure to include non-red garnets in your collection. Garnets have a lot more to offer than just earthen red.

Opal	An ancient and highly revered stone, today the better quality hails mainly from Australia. Most prized: **Australian Black Opal** Prized Origin: Lightning Ridge, Australia. Other Popular Opals: Crystal Opal, Mexican Fire Opal, Boulder Opal, African Opal, Jelly Opal, and Peruvian Opal. Their appearances vary from the traditional white opal (known as **"crystal"** opal) to the solid pastel blues of the Peruvian to the fiery cherry-red of the Mexican variety. ** Beware of Boulder Opal doublets and triplets. There's nothing wrong with them – they simply are not whole opals. Doublets and triplets have solid stone backings that give support to the thin layer of genuine opal affixed to them. Doublets and Triplets can be pretty, but they are generally a lot less expensive than a whole opal gemstone.

Pearls	These precious gems deserve an entire chapter to themselves. Suffice to say, if looking for the best, stick to: South Sea and Tahitian, _natural_ with _natural color_ and _round_ in shape. The larger the pearl (in circumference), the more it will cost. Prized Colors: **Yellow** and **Black**. Black pearls often have a "**peacock**" green hue to them. The "peacock" term is used to describe the rainbow of colors displayed by a natural iridescence given off by a thick, high-quality nacre (skin) on the pearls...and this display of color actually imbues the pearl with a deep green tone. The yellow South Sea pearls should have a true powdered golden yellow color. Akoya pearls are cultivated in oysters in the ocean (ie. in saltwater). They are more expensive than their freshwater cousins. **Akoya** pearls traditionally come in candlelight and eggshell off-white shades. Both cultured (cultivated in either fresh or salt water) and natural pearls have their benefits. It depends upon your needs, desires, and price point. Anything _not_ round in shape diminishes the cost of the pearl...although there are lots of other shapes that have become popular in jewelry – such as button, baroque, mabé, keshi, and coin pearls. ** Beware of dyed pearls. Color treating pearls by dying them is considered to lessen their value.

Ruby	Prized Origin: Burma Prized Color: **Lipstick Red with neon pink** flashes or overtones. Should have minimal inclusions, although rubies are naturally included. Try to find one as clean and inclusion-free as possible. Also Popular: African Rubies – They tend to be "pigeon blood red" (darker, more blood red) with *no* neon pink glow. ** Beware of glass-filled, enhanced, and synthetic stones.

Sapphire	Prized Origin: Kashmir, India (no longer available), and Sri Lanka (known as "Ceylon" until 1972) Comes in a rainbow of colors. Most prized hues in jewelry: perfect royal blue, pink, padparadscha, and yellow. Perfect Blue: known as "Kashmir Blue," is a rich, glowing royal blue. Its depth is magnificent and gives the gem a velvety sense. The closest shade to Kashmir known today is **"Ceylon Blue."** Ceylon Blue sapphires exhibit vibrant royal blue gem tones, and they are stunning and extremely valuable. Another popular shade of blue that has good market value today is a lighter, medium blue (a sky blue) shade called **"Cornflower Blue."** **"Padparadscha"** is very rare, and it's a perfect blend of pink and orange. In fact, it appears vibrantly peachy. However, it *cannot* be a pink sapphire with orange tones or an orange sapphire with pinkish coloring. It must be a consistent perfect pinkish-orange blended shade that saturates the entire gem with its perfectly peachy hue. ** Note: over 90% of sapphires have been heat-treated. This is common practice and is considered an aid in enhancing the gem's color. If you find a natural sapphire, *NOT* heat treated, it will be much more valuable, especially if the color is vivid, intense, and consistent throughout the entire gem.

Spinel	Comes in a variety of colors. All are valuable. **Hot Pink** is currently the most demanded although blue, red and purple are also exceptional. In fact, red spinel has often been mistaken for the finest of rubies. Spinel is never heated or treated in any way by man. It's one of the world's most stunning 100% natural gemstones, untouched by man's enhancements (other than to be shaped and polished). ** Beware of synthetics being passed off as genuine. Ask for GIA certification if needed.

Any gemstone that has survived the eons and still pleases man is remarkable. Other similar gems that have been time tested and are still in demand are:

Lapis Lazuli	Topaz	Carnelian
Turquoise	Agate	Onyx
Jade	Jasper	Coral

COLLECTOR STONES

As described above with the "Rule Breakers," there are many gemstones that people purchase with the hopes that stones' monetary value will increase over time; thus, the gems will eventually become good investments.

As previously stated, **we are not licensed to, nor do we assume to, give you any financial advice regarding gemstone investments or jewelry purchases**. The statements made in SAVVY are based purely on modern gemstone marketplace history, on recent pricing trends and from observing the value of certain scarce gems as they continue to increase over the years…especially as those stones become more and more rare. Simply put: the worth of these jewels typically continues to increase as the availability of these gems continues to decrease. It's basic supply and demand for gemstones that are no longer easily obtained.

That said, here is a brief list of gemstones that we know many collectors strive to add to their collections. These stones have continued to go up in monetary worth over the past several years. Why? Because they're becoming more and more scarce and are harder to find in good quality and/or in sufficient quantity.

Keep in mind, our suggestions are for *quality gems only*. Per evaluation using the "4 C" standards, any of these jewels (if of high quality) should be worth adding to anyone's collection.

Grab 'em while you can. The mines are running low or have recently closed!
- MANDARIN GARNET
- TANZANITE (especially from Blocks A & B of the mine)
- TANZANIAN PINK SPINEL
- RHODOCHROSITE (from Sweet Home Mine in Colorado)
- MUZO MINE EMERALDS (from Columbia)
- SLEEPING BEAUTY TURQUOISE (from the Sleeping Beauty mine in Globe, Arizona)

Grab these *if* you can. These are one source gems or are hard to source (due to weather conditions, governmental embargos, limited access to mines, and overall rarity of the stones).
- RUSSIAN ALEXANDRITE
- DEMANTOID GARNET (Russian)
- TSAVORITE GARNET (2.0 carats or larger)
- BURMESE Gemstones – especially RUBY and JADE
- BLUE ZIRCON (from Cambodia)
- WHITE SAPPHIRE
- PINK SAPPHIRE

- PADPARADSCHA SAPPHIRE
- COPPER BEARING TOURMALINE (African)
- PINK COPPER BEARING TOURMALINE
- AFRICAN CHROME TOURMALINE

The "extinct" (mined out) prized gemstones below are an absolute must if you're a collector.

- PARAIBA TOURMALINE (from Paraiba, Brazil)
- KASHMIR SAPPHIRE

** Note: Paraiba (pronounced "pahrah-eeba") tourmaline should come from Paraiba, Brazil. You may hear of a tourmaline being called "African Paraiba" because it has characteristics and a chemical make-up similar to a true Brazilian Paraiba, but African Paraibas are really African Copper Bearing Tourmaline. Copper Bearing Tourmaline are also highly valuable and are collectible, but they are not nearly as rare (or worth as much) as a true Brazilian Paraiba. In SAVVY, we refer to Paraiba Tourmaline as the original tourmaline that comes only from Paraiba, Brazil.

*** Note: if you ever come across a true Kashmir blue sapphire, certified as such, and you can afford it, add it to your collection. A blue Kashmir sapphire of highest quality is considered to be the "crème de la crème" of the jewelry world.

AUTHOR'S NOTE:
The glory days of the Kashmir mine were in the late 1800's. By the early 1900's, and certainly by World War I, the mine was closed. For the last century, very little has been done with it.

In modern history, there has been a common trend in gemstone mining: when a beautiful, high quality stone is discovered, there tends to be a lifespan on it. At first, it's introduced to the world and is oftentimes given a memorable and marketable name. It's sold at a fair market price until the demand for it outpaces its availability. Eventually, the flow of the gem into the marketplace slows, and this is caused either by natural or man-made factors. The mineral could be mined completely out, or other extraneous and political elements may prematurely force the mine's closure. When this happens, the gemstones are suddenly and abruptly no longer available to the market. And the moment this occurs, the value of those gemstones, along with their prices, soars…and often, this is seemingly overnight.

With many of our cited examples in SAVVY, the lifespan of a gem's mine tends to be only a few decades. Then when the mine does close, that gemstone disappears completely off the market. This can, and often does, cause an immediate sharp rise in demand for that particular jewel. And by the time word gets out about the mine's closure, there's often a feeding frenzy for that specific gem…and its value inevitably sky-rockets; and what was once a collector's stone suddenly becomes a rare jewel.

Recent examples of this type of gemstone frenzy have involved Mandarin Garnet, Paraiba Tourmaline, Copper Bearing Tourmaline, Fancy Pink Diamonds, and even cobalt blue (high quality) Tanzanite.

*AUTHOR'S NOTE:
SAVVY's main focus in this book is on colored gems. Why? Because diamonds are plentiful. Fancy pinks, yellows, and other natural diamond colors do add rarity and extreme value to those jewels. But generally speaking, white/colorless diamonds are extremely plentiful on this Earth. So for the sake of our savvy exotic gemstone aficionados, we've purposefully stayed mindful of the more rare and wondrous world of colored gemstones.

And now that you're becoming an instant connoisseur of colorful exotic gems, what do you put them in? How should you secure them so that you can wear them as fine jewelry?

Easy answer: in precious metals.

7 – PRECIOUS METALS

Precious Metals

Jewelry can be created out of virtually any material. However, the rarest, most reflective and hypoallergenic metals are used for fine jewelry. Although we give Titanium an honorable mention in this chapter, know that it's traditionally not considered a precious metal. Its popularity (especially in men's jewelry) has risen over the years; and because of that, we decided to include it here. Titanium has certainly become popular enough to warrant a special mention.

This list below showcases the highest quality, most common precious metals used in fine jewelry today:

GOLD – 14K, 18K and higher

STERLING SILVER – made with 92.5% pure silver (stamped as .925)

PLATINUM – the most precious of the precious!

PALLADIUM – platinum's sister, lighter weight and rarer

[RHODIUM – platinum's cousin, the Enforcer!]

GOLD

14K gold contains 58.5% pure gold. The remaining 41.5% is an alloy metal, which is mixed with the naturally soft precious metal to give it added strength and durability.

18K gold is 75% pure gold. The rest is alloy.

22K gold is almost 100% pure gold (24K is 100% pure gold), and therefore it is extremely soft and pliable. It will bend easily and will be much more delicate when used in jewelry.

Also, the higher the pure gold content of the metal, the richer and truer its golden color will be. Hence 22K gold appears more golden and "richer" than both 18K and 14K. And 18K definitely has a markedly more golden tone than the lighter yellow 14K metal.

Gold is typically offered in Yellow, White and Rose colors. The varying hues are created by using different metals in their alloy mixtures. Alloys are often made using a blend of copper, zinc, silver, and/or palladium. Throughout the years, other colors of gold (such as green) have been introduced to the market, but rose, white, and yellow remain steadfastly popular.

White gold is often enhanced with a Rhodium coating.

There are many reasons to choose either 14K or 18K gold. Your decision may be dependent upon the price. The difference between 14K and 18K could easily cost $1,000. Because 18K gold (75% pure gold) contains more pure gold than 14K (58.5% pure gold), 18K gold is substantially more costly than 14K. However, your decision should also depend upon the durability of the piece.

Are you hard on your jewelry?
Will you wear your ring daily for everyday activities?

If so, then you may want to consider 14K gold because it is much more durable and can withstand more aggressive wear. (Remember, about half of 14K gold is a strong metal alloy that gives the gold added strength and durability). Because of this, it is often highly recommended that men wear 14K regardless of what they can afford. 14K can suit an active man's lifestyle much better than a softer 18K gold.

But if your life is calmer and you're more careful with your jewelry, then 18K can offer an added depth and richness...and a subtle sophistication...that 14K cannot.

** Note: 10K gold is also available. Its pure gold content is only 41.7%, which means that almost 60% of the metal is something else. Because of this, SAVVY does not consider 10K gold a precious metal. However, it is very durable, and it's a good consideration for someone who is very hard on his/her jewelry. By the way, 10K gold with its 41.7% pure gold content is the lowest ratio of pure gold to alloy mix that is allowed in the United States to technically be designated as "gold." Any golden enhanced metal with less than 10K should not be referred to as "gold" in the US.

PLATINUM

Platinum is naturally an extremely white metal. It also has high reflectivity, which gives it immense shine. It is also heavy, dense, and strong, which makes it great for jewelry-making. If you have a prized center stone in a ring, holding it in place with platinum prongs (instead of gold) gives your jewel added security because platinum offers a much stronger hold. It's also much denser than gold, which means that an equally thin strip of platinum will retain its shape and strength much better than a thin strip of gold. Because of this, many luxury jewelers prefer to set their rings with heads consisting of platinum prongs.

And because platinum is a heavier metal than gold, a platinum ring will feel heftier on the finger than a gold ring. Some people like this feeling. The added heft of the jewelry makes it feel more luxurious. Once accustomed to the weight of platinum, many people are challenged to wear jewelry that does not offer the same substantial weightiness. They begin to associate this heftiness as an attribute of luxury…and as an indicator of quality.

Platinum that is used in jewelry is typically very pure, usually 95% pure or better. So when considering a platinum piece, rest assured knowing that your platinum is truly platinum (with few additives).

Because of the many positive attributes of platinum, along with the fact that it's a rare metal, it is expensive as compared to gold. In fact, the same setting offered in gold can be twice as expensive when set in platinum. Platinum is a costly precious metal to choose, but platinum does have intrinsic value, it secures gemstones better, and it retains its worth. It also holds its shape, resists scratching, and is naturally hypo-allergenic (good for all skin types). It also resists tarnishing, does not oxidize, and retains its shiny luster. It's a low-maintenance, high-worth rare and precious metal.

For these many reasons, platinum remains the metal of choice for the most luxurious jewelry pieces.

SILVER

Silver may surprise you. Like platinum, it is also a naturally white metal; but most people don't realize that it is the most reflective of all the precious metals. What does that mean? It means that sterling silver will outshine its counterparts, appearing whiter and brighter than the other white metals.

However, the challenge with silver is its softness. It's naturally softer than platinum, titanium, and even gold. Because of this, it's recommended that silver jewelry be best utilized in earrings, necklaces, and in bracelets. Silver is not advised for rings that are going to be worn every day. And silver is prone to oxidation (turning black); therefore, it will require regular cleanings.

Sterling silver is considered fine silver. Its pure silver content is 92.5% pure silver (which is why you'll see the .925 stamp on sterling silver jewelry). The other 7.5% alloy mixture is usually made of copper, giving the pliable silver metal some added stability and strength. This is needed to ensure that the jewelry will retain its shape for as long as possible.

RHODIUM

Rhodium is another white metal, and it is typically used to enhance the shine of white jewelry. Oftentimes rhodium is plated on top of a soft base metal (such as white gold and silver) rather than being used as the base metal itself. Rhodium plating gives a highly lustrous shine and an increased brilliance to your jewelry while also adding a layer of protection to it.

Rhodium is a cousin to platinum, and it offers similar attributes of strength and shine when it's employed in jewelry-making.

Many white gold and silver rings are actually rhodium plated to add a whiter, more brilliant shine to the metal. (Without rhodium plating, white gold often has a grayish appearance). The rhodium plating also protects the soft precious metals from scratches – but be aware that the rhodium will eventually wear off. After a year or more of wearing your jewelry, you may want to consider re-plating your rings with rhodium.

Although rhodium has many of the preferred properties of platinum, it's not as costly as platinum.

Conversely, rhodium can also be used to darken metals, thus giving some jewelry settings a "black" hue and an aged appeal. This blackened background usually sets off colored gemstones with stunning contrast, causing the gems' colors to be extra striking in appearance. Designers often use this black rhodium method to add depth and pleasing effects to their fashionable and stylized pieces.

TITANIUM

Titanium is a natural element that is whitish in color. Sometimes it can appear more silver or grey. In recent years, it has become increasingly popular in jewelry (especially in men's jewelry) for several reasons:

- It's the hardest natural metal in the world
- It has three times the strength of steel
- It's much stronger than all the other precious metals, but it's also much lighter weight
- Pure titanium is 100% hypoallergenic, which means it's great against all skin types
- It's more scratch-resistant than all the other precious metals
- When mixed with alloys, it can offer a wider variety of colors

The only negative with titanium is that if it ever needs to be cut off the finger in case of an emergency, it's extremely difficult to cut.

Also be aware that because of titanium's incredible strength, titanium rings are not sizable. Make sure the ring you choose fits your finger.

PALLADIUM

Palladium is a metal that falls into the same grouping as platinum. Palladium's fortés are that it's white, reflective, and super strong.

It's also one of the rarest metals in the world, rarer than platinum, and it's lighter weight than platinum. That's a plus for many jewelry wearers who want all the benefits of platinum but don't particularly want the heft of a platinum piece.

When used in jewelry, just as with platinum, palladium is 95% pure. It's extremely durable. And as with platinum and titanium, it's hypoallergenic and will not tarnish. It can remain white forever. It also has a superior ability to withstand corrosion and oxidation, which means it does not require another metal (like rhodium) to plate it. You won't have to clean it or maintain it like you would with gold or silver.

Similar to platinum, palladium offers the wearer myriad benefits.

However, palladium has rivaled platinum over the years as being one of the most expensive metals on Earth. For reasons of cost and scarcity, palladium is still used less than the other precious metals in jewelry manufacturing.

When you come across palladium jewelry, expect to pay higher prices for it. For all the right reasons, it can be viewed with the same high regard as platinum – palladium is the epitome of luxury!

ALTERNATIVE METALS

You may come across these alternative base metals as you shop. They all have their positive attributes and are used in fashion jewelry, but they're not regarded as precious.

10k Gold (any color)
Tungsten Carbide
Stainless Steel
Pewter
Copper
Bronze
Brass

ALLOY METALS

These metals are generally used in various alloy mixtures:

Silver, palladium, copper, zinc, brass, bronze, pewter, titanium, mokume-gane, stainless steel, and tungsten.

** Note: Nickel was once a favored ingredient for alloys used to create white gold; but so many people had severe allergic reactions to nickel that many manufacturers no longer use nickel as a part of their alloy mixtures.

ALTERNATIVE MATERIALS

Jewelry is literally made from any material on Earth. Most jewelry throughout the eons has been made from beautiful natural minerals (rocks and gemstones) or something organic that came from a living organism, such as a fossil, shell or an animal part.

But with modern man's ability to create plastics, resins, gels, glass and other lab-generated concoctions, these artificial materials have found their ways into department store jewelry. These synthetics are generally only found in costume jewelry and are not considered fine or luxurious by any SAVVY or jewelry industry standards.

Think creatively. Here is a list of alternative organic materials that have been used throughout history and in different cultures around the globe to create beautiful, artistic jewelry:

Mother of Pearl
Abalone Shell
Coral
Nuts (such as highly polished Tagua Nut)
Wood (such as jet, a fossilized wood, or Paulo Santo, the only known wood so dense that it does not float in water)
Leathers – especially exotic leather such as sting ray skin
Bone
Amber
Rabbits Feet
Feathers
Ivory
Teeth
Animal Claws (bear & big cats)
Spiny Oyster Shell

MODERN ORGANIC and MINERAL ALTERNATIVES

These are currently often used as center or accent stones:

Russian Chariote
Sponge Coral
Jelly Opal
Chalcedony
Oxblood Coral
Sodalite
Sugilite
Ammolite
Fluorite
Agate

This list could continue indefinitely. The point is that jewelry can – and is – still typically made of any natural, Mother Nature created, mineral or organic material deemed beautiful and that adds status to the wearer.

** Note: however, by this author's own definition and according to the industry's sense of 'fine jewelry' – and for the sake of our quick connoisseurs – remember that true luxury jewelry is created with quality diamonds and/or natural color gemstones that receive high grades according to the "4 C" standards and then are set in precious metals.

8 – CLEANING & CARE

Jewelry Cleaning and Care

Jewelry maintenance is simple. If ever in doubt, you can go online and follow instructions listed on hundreds of websites. But basically, it boils down to simple common sense: put your jewelry on *after* you have applied your hairspray and make-up, and don't wear your jewelry during activities that may get it dirty (such as while gardening or exercising). Dirt, perspiration, and body oils can collect on or in between your gemstones and wear them down or stain them. Clean your jewelry regularly following some of the basic suggestions below. And take them annually to a trusted jeweler, who can clean and polish them (and possibly re-string them) professionally for you.

BASIC HOME MAINTENANCE

For **faceted hard gemstones** (such as sapphires and diamonds):

Soak them in a mild dishwashing detergent and use a soft toothbrush for a light scrub. Rinse thoroughly in clean water.

For **soft, porous gems** (such as turquoise and pearls):

Wipe them with a soft cloth or chamois.

DO NOT soak them in dish soap. It will ruin their luster and perhaps even eat away at their organic material. Avoid using anything rough or abrasive on these gems as their surfaces will tend to scratch. Paper towels and toothbrushes are too tough for them.

BEST ADVICE:

Use specialized cloths designed for cleaning gems, pearls, or precious metals.

Periodically take your jewelry to be cleaned and polished professionally by your trusted jeweler.

When not wearing it, store your fine jewelry in softly lined, dark boxes or jewelry bags. Keep your colored stones away from intense direct sunlight.

9 – APPENDICES

For quick charts and easy reference, the following appendices are designed for you to find everything from the ideal, most highly prized color of each gemstone to fun facts and lore related to today's more popular jewels.

APPENDIX A

Optimal Stone Colors

Colors should be intense and consistent throughout the entire stone. There should be no "gaps" in color or obvious serious fading of color. If the stone contains areas of missing color (where it's clear or extremely faded), that's called "color zoning;" and that's not a good thing. Color zoning that erases the gem's color and leaves it colorless at any angle actually decreases the value of the gem by quite a bit.

So look for gems with consistent and intense color (at all angles) throughout the entire stone. Consistency and intensity are key!

Gemstone Color Name or Origin	Color Description
Amethyst	
Siberian (Russian) or Uruguayan	Richest, velvety deep royal purple with flashes of blue and red
Aquamarine	
Santa Maria Aquamarine	Perfect "swimming pool blue" color
Citrine	
Madeira	The richest amber golden yellow of sunset (could also be the magnificent goldens of late autumn leaves)
Coral	
Sardinian (and other Mediterranean)	Vibrant Fire Engine Red. Rich coloring with no striations or variations in depth of color. No visible markings or blemishes scarring the coral.

Salmon	Intense, Rich Pink-Peach color. Often carved to highlight the subtle variations and strata of colors within the coral.
Angel Skin	Pastel, Soft Pink. It can pale towards white and darken towards salmon pink, but the overall color tone is a soft, powder pink. Often carved to show off the subtle colorations within the coral.
Black Coral	Not as well known. Is often confused with onyx because polished black coral has a similar look to polished black onyx. However, black coral can have growth patterns (similar to a tree's rings) that subtly add nice texture and personality to the coral. Some black coral has brownish markings, and those are coral "mutations," natural to the coral. Sometimes those mutations are used to enhance a piece and to add significance to a black coral carving. Look for flashes of red "fire" within a polished piece. This "fire" adds unique depth, personality and character to the coral. ** Author's Note: Many of these corals are highly monitored by government and international agencies because they are protected natural species. As such, the supply for the jewelry industry has been limited in order to protect and preserve the living coral. As you find these corals in luxury jewelry stores, please know

	that the coral has likely been harvested and obtained through fully legal, authorized and sanctioned means.
Emerald	
Columbian Emerald	Deep jungle green with neon green flashes or overtones.
* Muzo Mine Emerald (from Columbia)	Regarded as the most prized color: richest, deepest Amazon greens offset by vibrant lime and neon green overtones. The emerald can appear to "glow" from the inside out.
Garnet	
Anthill Garnet (from Arizona)	Blood or cabernet red with nice transparency. Looks liquid beneath the surface.
Demantoid Garnet	Subtle olivine green with an overtone of forest green and a layer of dancing neon and electric lime green brilliance.
Green Grossular Garnet	Lively springtime green with lime overtones.
Hessonite Garnet	Orange brown garnet resembling the color of cinnamon.
Mandarin Garnet	Electric orange with tangerine overtones. It glows with "fire" from the inside out. Radiates like the sun.

Rhodolite Garnet	Vibrant glowing Kool-Aid red perfection with velvety depth.
Spessartite Garnet	Burnt orange, almost brown. It's the base color for the mandarin garnet, just without the tangerine overtones.
Tsavorite Garnet	The perfect Amazonian green of Summer. Every emerald wishes it could be this rich and clean.
Jade	
Imperial Jade	Vibrant forest green, the perfect crayon green.
Lavender Jade	Rich lavender purple, not too white.
Moonstone	
Blue Moonstone	Sky blue tint overrides the milky white base color.
Peach Moonstone	Soft peach overrides the creamy base color.
Opal	
Black Opal (from Lightning Ridge, Australia)	Base color appears to be more of a dark blue than black. The best jewels have vibrant gemstone colors emitting from the entire opal in regular repeated patterns with a predominance of red and orange "fire."
Crystal Opal	Also known by many as "white" opal. It's the more traditional opal Americans are

	familiar with. It has a creamy base color that is accented with flashes of color throughout the entire stone. Most prized stones have a consistent pattern of multi-colors throughout the entire gem with a predominance of red, orange, blue and green flashes.
Mexican Fire Opal	The best quality gems are almost as red as ruby. They glow from the inside out. Can be electric cherry red. ** Note: fire opals should not be too orange, pale, or cloudy (opaque).
Peruvian Opal	A chalky opaque blue, reflecting the early morning sky. Almost a powdery consistency. ** Note: some Peruvian opal can be powdery pink as well.
Pearls	
Akoya	Akoya pearls are cultured pearls, cultivated in oysters in the ocean (in salt water). Akoyas are more expensive than their freshwater cousins. They generally come in an eggshell or candlelight off-white color.
Black	The base nacre color is such a rich black that the luster of the nacre (skin of the pearl) is luxurious. It can often appear to be more pewter in its tone. ** Note: the South Seas and Tahiti are known to produce the best black pearls.

Golden	Golden yellow depth within the nacre and a perfect orientation of each pearl gives it a candlelight shimmer reminiscent of the candle's flame or powdered gold. ** Note: the South Seas and Tahiti are known to produce the best specimens.
Peacock	It's a black pearl whose luster creates so much color that the pearl looks like it has more of a deep greenish hue, and it reflects a rainbow of colors off its rich lustrous surface. ** Note: the South Seas and Tahiti are considered to produce the best.
Peridot	
Pakistani Peridot	Neon glowing electric green.
Rhodochrosite	
Sweet Home Mine Rhodochrosite (from Colorado)	Electric neon pink, as alive and vibrant as pink ever wanted to be.
Ruby	
Burmese Ruby	Vibrant lipstick red, sometimes leaning towards blood red, with hot neon pink overtones.
Sapphire	
Blue Sapphire: Ceylon Blue	Deepest royal velvety blue, the next

	best thing to Kashmir blue.
Cornflower Blue	An appealing medium sky blue, also a popular shade.
Kashmir Blue	Deepest glowing royal blue with a palpable velvety texture. Blue perfection with such a royal tone that the color glows from the depths of the gem. This perfect medium royal blue emanates from deep within the jewel and radiates lively intensity from the inside out.
** Note: blue sapphires should be strikingly blue. They should NOT appear black at a glance. They should be evidently blue even from across a room.	
Padparadscha Sapphire	Padparadscha is a perfect blend of pink and orange, oftentimes appearing vibrantly peachy. "Padparadscha" is derived from the Sanskrit word for "lotus blossom," the color it is thought most closely to resemble.
** Note: it will NOT be a true padparadscha if it is an orange sapphire with a pinkish tone or a pink sapphire with some orange coloring. The entire stone itself must be a pure, consistent blend of the	

ideal pink and orange hues. If it looks predominantly pink (or orange) then it will be classified as a pink (or orange) sapphire, not a "padparadscha."

Pink Sapphire

** Note: pink sapphires are scarce on the market and are hard to find in good quality. Grab one if you find one you love!

The perfect shade of bubblegum pink. It can also cast a neon or electric glow.

Yellow Sapphire

The most vibrant lemon yellow of sunny afternoon skies. Also, it can be the perfect crayon yellow with electricity pumping through it.

Tanzanite	
"Dark Super Neon" (darkest cobalt blue with piercing neon blues that emanate at times. It appears electrified) ** Note: tanzanite is now	Deepest cobalt blue with flashes of royal purple and red. ** Note: tanzanite from Block D is the most recently mined. It also produces the least amount of saturated color in the stones. Generally speaking, your richer, better colors were mined first, from Blocks A, B, & C.

often seen in a periwinkle blue (soft powdery shade of blue with lavender traits). Periwinkle blue tanzanite (or other colors such as green tanzanite) are not valued nearly as highly as the deep, dark, original cobalt blue tanzanite.	
Topaz	
Imperial Topaz	Peachy honey color with strong red overtones, usually at the "ends" and/or edges of the stone.
London Blue Topaz	Dark, calming blue. Rich in depth like a deep ocean.
Sky Blue Topaz	Opposite of London Blue. Glows brilliantly like the sky on a perfect summer's day.
Swiss Blue Topaz	Neon electric sky blue. Dazzling and piercing. It often incorporates both the darker elements of the London Blue and the vibrance of the Sky Blue. Swiss blue is electric and exciting.
Turquoise	
Green (from the American Southwest and Arizona)	Muddled varieties of earth-tone greens. Often the matrix is prominent within each stone.

Purple (from the American Southwest. Popular varieties come from Kingman, Arizona, and the Mojave Desert. Often referred to as "Mojave Turquoise")	Muddled shades of lavender and purple. Its matrix and complimentary elements (such as copper) oftentimes add uniqueness and personality to each piece.
Sleeping Beauty Blue – also known as "Robin Egg Blue" (Persia is thought to produce the highest quality blue turquoise)	Considered turquoise perfection! This is the ideal turquoise blue that resembles the shallow waters of the Caribbean Ocean. It's most valued when it's pure and consistent in color, without any of the matrix included in the gem; however, the "matrix" (black markings of complimentary elements naturally occurring in and around the gemstone) sometimes remains in the polished stone, and that adds unique personality to each piece.
Zircon	
Blue Zircon (Best quality comes from Cambodia)	Extremely brilliant rich teal color. It's electric teal!
Cognac Zircon	Perfect brown of a good cognac liquor. Careful, it may cause you to crave a Cuban cigar!
Red Zircon	Vibrant cabernet red with brilliant electric red "sparks."

APPENDIX B

Diamond Grading

Color:

Diamond color is graded on an alphabetical scale. The higher in the alphabet (closer to A), the better. The grading starts at D (there is no A, B or C), with D being the best colorless diamond possible. Then it moves down the alphabet incrementally from there.

GIA Grade	Color
D E F	Colorless
G H	Near Colorless
I J	Near Colorless, Slight Tint Starting
K L M	Slightly Tinted (usually yellowish or brown hue)
N O P Q R	Very Light Yellow (sometimes appears tan)
S - Z	Light Yellow to Yellow or Brown

D-F Diamonds are the most luxurious, best quality colorless diamonds. They are usually available by request only. Reserved for the elite.

G-H Diamonds are typically on display in high-end jewelers. If someone tells you they use G color diamonds, that's a GOOD thing. In fact, it should be impressive.

I-J Diamonds are often found in moderate jewelry. I-J diamonds are very common. Someone with a trained eye will immediately spot I-J diamonds: compared to higher quality colorless diamonds, I-J stones tend to look a bit "dirtier" and "dingier."

With K color diamonds, most people can easily start to see some discoloration in the gem. That color may or may not be desired, depending on whether it leans towards a brownish hue or towards a brighter yellow ("fancy") color.

Fancy colored diamonds are rare and, if natural (untreated), are some of the most expensive gems on the planet.

** Note: fancy diamonds are found in a variety of colors. There are vibrant yellows, fierce pinks, fiery oranges, steel blues, misty greens, crisp champagnes, cool whites, and even coal blacks.

Color is a personal preference, but clarity definitely adds another critical dimension to your diamond's worth.

Clarity:

Clarity starts its scale at "Flawless" then works its way down toward highly "Included."

Clarity	Description
IF "Flawless"	Internally Flawless – otherwise known as "Flawless." Under 10X magnification, there are NO internal blemishes to be found
VVS 1	Very Very Slightly Included – the inclusions are extremely difficult to find under 10X magnification
VVS 2	Very Very Slightly Included – the inclusions are still difficult to find under 10X magnification
VS 1 & VS 2	Very Slightly Included – the inclusions and blemishes are hard to find under 10X magnification
SI 1 & SI 2	Slightly Included – the inclusions and blemishes are easy to spot under 10X magnification
I-1, I-2, & I-3	Included – The inclusions are easy to spot and are oftentimes obvious with the naked eye

Flawless diamonds are extremely rare and are extremely expensive. If a jeweler even has one, you will have to ask for it to be retrieved from the vault to be shown to you.

VVS diamonds are the cleanest diamonds commonly available on the market. These are the best quality diamonds you will find as both accent and center stones. The highest-end, luxury designers may use VVS diamonds exclusively in their jewelry collections.

VS diamonds are also considered high-end. Many times, designers will mix VS and VVS diamonds in their accent stones. It's a nice blend and is still considered luxurious.

In summary, VS-G diamonds (or better) are exceptional and are used by the highest quality jewelers.

SI diamonds are sometimes the highest quality stones that average jewelry stores will carry. Just know that they are common diamonds. There's typically nothing wrong with SI, it's just not highest end or luxurious. When dealing with an SI diamond, consider the color and carat weight as well. A nearly colorless SI-1 diamond can be beautiful, impressive, and expensive, especially if it's a larger carat weight. Remember, <u>carat</u> weight and <u>cut</u> are vitally important when evaluating diamonds.

I stones are cloudy and dull, yet many excited tourists have been fooled by vendors in bazaars hawking their "goods." If the stone you're admiring looks "dirty" or "dingy," or if you can plainly see black flecks or brown smears within the stone, they're likely I clarity or worse. Beware of your purchase. And always trust your eyes!

AUTHOR'S NOTE:

Clarity and color are extremely important when valuing a diamond, but don't forget that CARAT weight and CUT are the most prized attributes of a diamond. Please note that CUT does not mean its shape (ie. marquise, round, brilliant, emerald, princess, etc). A diamond's "cut" refers instead to the quality of its proportions, its symmetry, and its polish. How is its depth in proportion to its width? How do its angles on the pavilion work in symmetry with the angles of its crown? If the diamond is poorly cut (no matter what shape it is), it will have less brilliance (sparkle) than a diamond well cut. So even if you had a diamond with perfect clarity and color, if it was badly cut, your diamond wouldn't shine and scintillate like it should.

** Proper cutting is an absolute must with all of your gems, and it cannot be emphasized enough!

The finest, optimal cutting always enhances the best qualities in a gem.

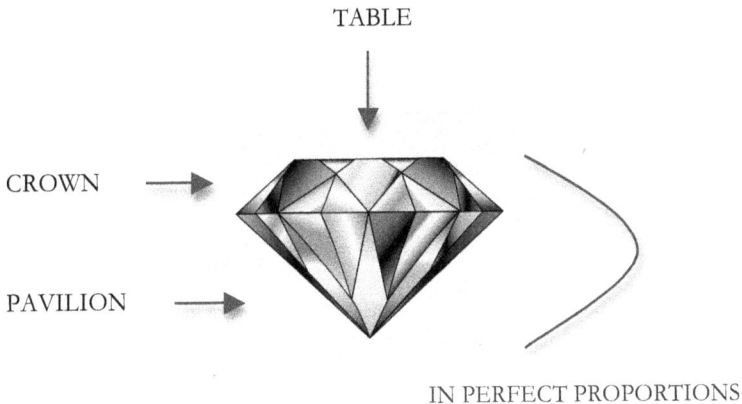

TABLE

CROWN ➡

PAVILION ➡

IN PERFECT PROPORTIONS

APPENDIX C

<u>Gem Shapes</u>

Gemstones can be cut into a variety of shapes, with traditional tools as well as with modern lasers. A stone's "cut" generally refers to the quality of its proportions and symmetry along with its polish. However, a gem's "shape" is the shape you see at a glance. There are many more shapes than the ones listed here, but this chart shows some of the most popular shapes available today.

OVAL	ROUND	CUSHION
MARQUISE	HEART	BAGUETTE
PEAR	PRINCESS	TRILLION

And there are infinite variations of the basic shapes. Some of the more popular are emerald, Portuguese round, round brilliant, cleftless heart, and free form.

Below is just a sampling of the many variations that an experienced lapidary (gemstone cutter) can create. From traditional to fancy to phenomenal, if the cutting is in proper proportions and is aligned along the correct axis of the stone, each individual shape can invite the light to dance through the gemstone in uniquely fluid and beautiful motions. Consequently, each gem will be brilliantly dazzling in its own special and unique way!

APPENDIX D

<u>Birthstones</u>

Month	Modern	Traditional	Alternatives
January	Garnet	Red Garnet	Other Colors of Garnet
February	Amethyst	Amethyst	Prasiolite
March	Aquamarine	Aquamarine	Morganite
April	Diamond	Diamond	White Zircon, White Sapphire, or Demantoid Garnet
May	Emerald	Emerald	Tsavorite Garnet or Red Beryl
June	Pearl or Moonstone	Pearl	Crystal Opal
July	Ruby	Ruby	Rubellite Tourmaline or Red Spinel

Month	Modern	Traditional	Alternatives
August	Peridot	Carnelian	Green Jade, Green Garnet, or Green Tourmaline
September	Blue Sapphire	Royal Blue Sapphire	Other Colors of Sapphire or Iolite (also known as the "Water Sapphire")
October	Crystal Opal	Jasper	Black Opal, Mexican Fire Opal, or Peruvian Opal
November	Yellow Topaz or Citrine	Citrine	Imperial Topaz
December	Blue Topaz, Blue Turquoise, or Tanzanite	Robin Egg Blue Turquoise or Blue Zircon	Lapis Lazuli

APPENDIX E

Anniversary & Commemorative Gemstones

Anniversary	Gemstone
1st	Gold
2nd	Garnet
3rd	Pearl
4th	Blue Topaz
5th	Blue Sapphire
6th	Amethyst
7th	Onyx
8th	Green Tourmaline
9th	Lapis Lazuli
10th	Diamond
11th	Turquoise
12th	Jade
13th	Citrine
14th	Opal
15th	Ruby
16th	Peridot
17th	Watches
18th	Cat's Eye Chrysoberyl
19th	Aquamarine
20th	Emerald

Anniversary	Gemstone
21st	Iolite
22nd	Spinel
23rd	Imperial Topaz
24th	Tanzanite
25th	Silver Jubilee
30th	Pearl Jubilee
35th	Emerald
40th	Ruby
45th	Sapphire
50th	Golden Jubilee
55th	Alexandrite
60th	Diamond Jubilee
70th	Sapphire Jubilee
80th	Ruby Jubilee

** Note: the 75th anniversary is often celebrated as a second Diamond Jubilee

APPENDIX F

The Mohs Scale

Developed by Friedrich Mohs in 1812, this scale is used to grade the hardness of minerals. Mohs made a list of ten separate minerals with varying degrees of hardness, and he compiled those minerals as the standard by which all other minerals would be graded. Whichever mineral scratches another is considered the "harder" one. If both minerals that are being compared scratch each other, they're considered to have equal hardness.

Thus the Mohs Scale is used to determine which stone is harder and which is softer, and it is used to determine which mineral can scratch another. Thus, the Mohs Scale is a *relative* way to measure and compare minerals. (Truth be known, a diamond, the hardest substance, in actuality is 4 times harder than a corundum and is 6 times harder than a topaz; but in the Mohs Scale, a diamond receives a score of 10 while the corundum is a 9 and topaz is an 8).

Author's Note:
Because gemstones do have different hardnesses and can be affected with scratches, chips, and dings, it is recommended that certain softer gemstones should only be used in jewelry pieces that are typically less exposed to damage, such as in pendants and earrings. When softer gems are used in rings, they need to be worn with care because they can be more readily chipped.

Gemstones worn in rings generally should rank 7 or higher on the Mohs Scale to ensure that they can withstand daily wear and tear.

The Mohs Scale of Mineral Hardness:

With 10 being the hardest mineral and 1 being the softest

Hardness	Mineral
10	Diamond
9	Corundum (Sapphire & Ruby)
8	Topaz
7	Quartz (Amethyst & Citrine)
6	Feldspar
5	Apatite
4	Fluorite
3	Calcite
2	Gypsum
1	Talc

* Note: the Mohs Scale does use ½-step measurements to grade minerals. For example, if a stone can scratch Apatite but not Feldspar, it would receive a grade of 5 ½.

Popular Gems and Their Mohs Hardness:

Gem	Hardness
Diamond	10
Ruby	9
Sapphire	9
Alexandrite	8.5
Chrysoberyl	8.5
Spinel	8
Topaz	8
Emerald	7.5 – 8
Aquamarine	7.5 – 8
Morganite	7.5 – 8
Red Beryl	7.5 – 8
Chrome Tourmaline	7 – 7.5
Paraiba Tourmaline	7 – 7.5
Rubellite Tourmaline	7 – 7.5
Tourmaline	7 – 7.5
Danburite	7 – 7.5
Demantoid Garnet	7 – 7.5
Iolite	7 – 7.5
Garnets	6.5 – 7.5
Kunzite	7

Gem	Hardness
Quartz: Amethyst, Citrine, Ametrine, Prasiolite, All Colors	7
Agate	6.5 – 7
Bloodstone	6.5 – 7
Carnelian	6.5 – 7
Chalcedony	6.5 – 7
Fossil Coral	6.5 – 7
Jasper	6.5 – 7
Onyx	6.5 – 7
Peridot	6.5 – 7
Tanzanite	6.5 – 7
Rhodolite Garnet	6.5
Labradorite	6 – 6.5
Moonstone	6 – 6.5
Opal	5.5 – 6
Fire Opal	5.5 – 6
Chrome Diopside	5 – 6
Lapis Lazuli	5 – 6
Turquoise	5 – 6
Sphene	5 – 5.5
Apatite	5
Ammolite	4

Gem	Hardness
Fluorite	4
Rhodochrosite	4
Malachite	3.5 − 4
Coral	3 − 4
Pearl	2.5 − 4.5
Amber	2

APPENDIX G

Attributes & Lore

Below are some of the traditions and lore surrounding popular gemstones. Many of the oldest known, more established gems have rich histories mixed with intriguing mythology, professed health benefits, and unusual uses.

Alexandrite

It hails from the Chrysoberyl family of stones, and it has strong color change traits. Depending on the light it's in, it appears to morph between an earthen green and a blood red. Because of this phenomenal trait, an Alexandrite is said to be "an emerald by day and a ruby by night."

The Alexandrite was discovered in Russia in 1830 during the time of the czars. Because the stone displays both red and green characteristics – and the colors of imperial Russia were coincidentally red and green – this uniquely Russian gemstone was named for Czar Alexander II on the occasion of his coming of age.

Since its original nineteenth century discovery in the Ural mountains, Alexandrite has also been found in other places around the world, including in Sri Lanka, Zimbabwe, and Hematita, Brazil. However, Russian Alexandrite is still regarded as the most prized Alexandrite on the planet, especially when it displays high color change probability – of 80% or more.

Russian Alexandrite is one of the most rare...and therefore, most expensive...gemstones in the world. It is most definitely a collector's gem. Try to find one larger than 1.5 carats.

Amethyst

Purple has long been considered the most royal of colors. As such, a deep purple amethyst still receives the reverence and honor reserved for royalty.

Amethyst was an important and integral gem in decorating the Catholic Churches during the Middle Ages because it was believed to symbolize and encourage piety and celibacy. It was so revered for these traits that it was also used as the main gemstone in the ring of Bishops…and it's still used in a Bishop's band today.

The modern Tibetans consider amethyst to be sacred to Buddha, and rosaries are often created from the purple gem.

Leonardo Da Vinci wrote that the amethyst was able to dissipate evil thoughts and quicken intelligence.

The ancient Greeks considered amethyst to be a strong antidote to drunkenness, and they carved many drinking goblets from it, thinking this magical stone would enable them to enjoy more of their wine-infested Bacchanalia! Don't think the ancient Greeks are alone in this. Even today, many people around the globe will still attest that amethyst guards for sobriety.

Although the most prized color in amethyst is the deepest royal purple, a pale powdery lavender can also receive some prestige. This subtle color is affectionately referred to as the "Rose of France," and it was a favored hue in Victorian jewelry.

Aquamarine

Aquamarine, the light blue-green cousin to emerald, has a long history. Its popularity has remained high throughout the years although its prized color has changed with time. A century ago, the most valued tone was a light seafoam green color, reminiscent of the shallows of saltwater and the crests of ocean waves. Today, we prefer the cleaner, "pool water blue" hues that are so richly exemplified in stones that come from the Santa Maria mine in Brazil.

Aquamarine is attributed with having its own set of unique powers. It is said that aquamarine can help filter mental information and thereby aid in sharpening a person's perception. With enhanced mental acuity, the stone allegedly also assists with better and clearer communications.

Want to improve your public speaking skills? Wear this gem. Aquamarine is believed to enhance your verbal abilities as well.

In the more esoteric world: if you dream that you have an aquamarine (or you dream that you find one), it bodes well for a happy love life.

Emerald

Emerald is another gemstone that has been deeply revered and admired throughout the ages. Some of the earliest known emerald mines date back to ancient Egypt, from approximately 2,000 BCE. It is purported that the emerald was Cleopatra's favorite gem.

Emerald is thought to banish forgetfulness and to enhance your intuition. It is also believed that emerald can transmit wisdom from the ethereal (spiritual) plane to its wearer, and that that newfound wisdom can (and should) then be passed on to others.

Because of the mental strengths associated with emerald, it is believed that light green emeralds can assist in meditation. However, when its color is a deep jungle Amazonian green, the gem provides inspiration and encourages action.

As a whole, an emerald offers physical, emotional, spiritual, and mental balance.

Garnet

Garnets have a rich history. Ancient travelers used to carry garnets to protect against accidents while far from home. Ironically, and conversely, in both Asia and the American Southwest, garnets were sometimes used as bullets. It was believed that the vibrant red color of the garnet would increase the intensity of the wound it inflicted.

Many aged stories attribute the garnet with the ability to illuminate the night. Legend has it that Noah himself suspended a garnet in the ark in order to disperse light.

Red Garnet is also said to represent physical love. It's highly attuned to the heart's energy, and it can enhance passion. It also encourages a person to exercise self-control, especially of his/her anger towards oneself.

If you also want to control your fiery passions, try a red garnet. A garnet is about self-control.

Opal

Opal is a gemstone with a long history that is often thought to symbolize purity and love. It can often represent hope as well; and it fosters both love and faithfulness. Because of this, it was once the gem of choice for engagement rings.

In the esoteric realm: if you see opal in your dreams, it is said that you will receive great possessions.

It is purported that William Shakespeare coined the opal as the "Queen of Gems." In fiery, vibrant crystal and black opals (especially in jewels that display vivid, rich pin-fire patterns), every color under the rainbow can be seen dancing within the opal. Perhaps that's why she's considered the queen – she embodies characteristics of all the other gems.

Fire Opal is believed to be good for business. Wear this hot, cherry red gem to enhance your commercial success.

Ruby

As one of the oldest, most treasured jewels throughout the ages, the ruby has been desired for eons. Stone age tools found in Burma indicate that rubies have been mined there for thousands of years.

The fiery intense red of ruby, as you might imagine, is believed to foster deep passions. Along with those intense emotions come romance and marriage. Its energy is positive, and it helps with all matters related to love and lust…including increasing virility!

Revered over the centuries by royalty, rubies are gems that

traditionally symbolize leadership. It's a strong stone for males to wear, promoting vitality, excessive energy, strength, virility and wealth.

On ladies, it is regarded as a symbol of love and unbridled passion. It can signify power, too; and the ruby can symbolize her strength and personal fortitude.

On a man, the ruby indicates power and authority. It is indeed the stone of kings!

Sapphire

Blue sapphire symbolizes loyalty, purity and truth. It also represents divine favor; and because of this, blue sapphire is the gemstone of choice for high priests and royalty.

Because it is also known to represent enduring faithfulness and sincerity, it has also been a favored gem for use in engagement rings. Prince Charles gave Lady Diana Spencer the infamous royal blue oval sapphire that the Duchess of Cambridge, Kate Middleton, now proudly wears.

It's a stone of healing, and deep blue sapphire is thought to bring peace and serenity to its wearer.

Yellow Sapphire has its own traditions, and it can be associated with the Hindu god of prosperity, Ganesh. Yellow sapphire is said to attract wealth to its wearer. Just be sure to wear it with the gem touching your skin.

Yellow sapphire can also stimulate the intellect as it helps with focus. It's a good gem for the keen mind.

Tanzanite

Tiffany & Co introduced Tanzanite to the world in 1969. It was intended to be a substitute and replacement for the royal blue Kashmir Sapphire.

It's such a "new" gemstone in the marketplace that it hasn't had much time to gain lore. However, it has had more of an impact on the world of gemstones than any other jewel discovered in modern history. It has definitely had a lasting effect on the market and has made a huge splash in the jewelry world.

No other gemstone has seen such acceptance, uptake and increased monetary value as the original cobalt blue, especially the "dark super neon," tanzanite extracted from Blocks A & B of the mine.

Tourmaline

It's America's official national gemstone, and it has been discovered in over 30,000 different hues. It's truly a "rainbow" gem, known to come in every imaginable color.

Pink Tourmaline is frisky! It encourages the loss of inhibitions and the experience of enriched sexual pleasure. It's the aphrodisiac of the gemstone world!

Green Tourmaline, like a green traffic light, means "go." Green Tourmaline is said to encourage you to develop positive relationships. It also helps you deal constructively with problems, therefore it is the stone of choice to help you solve problems.

Watermelon Tourmaline, the mix of the pink and green tourmaline, is a stone which will do both: it will help you to solve problems while inviting love into a situation. Therefore, watermelon tourmaline is said to aid in amicable resolutions by bringing peace through mutual understanding.

Many other stones have their own unique lore, mythologies, and purported healing effects. If you're curious about other stones, a quick search on the Internet may provide you some intriguing information about your favorite gems.

For those of you more interested in the esoteric meanings of gems, you may wish to read through the many books written about crystal healing and associated medicinal uses.

APPENDIX H

<u>Bridal</u>

AUTHOR'S NOTE TO ENGAGED COUPLES:

Do what you want.

Whether you're traditional, conservative, contemporary, unique, artsy, or rebellious, do what suits you. We've heard too many brides talk about "tradition" while not really understanding what "tradition" truly is…or, frankly, what it means.

How traditional do you want to be? Or <u>*not*</u> to be?
What does "traditional" mean to you?

We've heard so many ladies speak of wanting a "traditional" diamond solitaire engagement ring, and we get it. We understand what they're saying because we, too, have been alive for the last several decades, and we've seen many giddy ladies cry when that gorgeous rock dons their left hands. We also understand that it's a widely accepted…and widely demanded…popular gesture for the groom-to-be to offer his bride-to-be a promissory diamond ring.

Thank you, De Beers!

Did you know that the diamond engagement ring has only risen in popularity during the last century? And that it was De Beers (the largest diamond conglomerate in the world) who so successfully marketed the diamond engagement ring? In fact, one could say that De Beers invented the diamond engagement ring and introduced it to modern society. Their marketing has been so successful and ubiquitous that the populace often accepts the company's marketing statements as 'facts:'

"A Diamond is Forever." True, but that phrase was first coined in 1947 by the marketing geniuses working for De Beers. Since then, the De Beers marketing department has continued its exemplary practice of creating new diamond wants and using advertising to instill these now common terms into our lexicon: "the eternity ring," "the past, present, and future" ring (also known as the "trilogy" ring), and the "right hand ring." Brilliant!

Truth be known, though, it wasn't De Beers who invented the concept of the diamond engagement ring. They just made it extremely popular and prolific in modern times. Throughout the Middle Ages, long before De Beers existed as a company, diamonds were a gem of choice, given as betrothing gifts by the wealthy. Because of the diamond's exquisite beauty, heavenly brilliance, and extreme durability, royalty and the elite (those who could afford such gems) used the diamond as a way to symbolize their enduring love. However, in the last century, it is De Beers who has used their marketing prowess to impress upon Western society's psyche the need for a diamond engagement ring. And thanks to the Industrial Revolution and the rise of the Middle Class, there were many new customers ready and willing to purchase that elusive sparkling gem that was once the exclusive domain of the elite!

However, there are many examples throughout history of other gemstones being the supreme choice for engagement gifts and promissory jewelry. For example, Prince Charles chose to give Lady Diana Spencer an incredible blue sapphire as her promise ring. After all, sapphires symbolize purity, loyalty and faithfulness. In turn, Prince William, Charles and Diana's eldest son, gave his betrothed, Kate Middleton, this same beloved family heirloom. Interestingly, Prince Andrew, the younger brother of Prince Charles, gave his fiancée, Sarah Ferguson, a colored engagement ring as well. Hers was a pigeon blood red ruby. Her ring embodied passion, power, and prowess.

Even earlier in the twentieth century, in 1936, the Duke of Windsor, Edward VIII, proposed to his beloved Wallis Simpson with a 19.77 carat rectangular cut emerald set in platinum. When they wed a year later, the American-born Simpson received a "marriage contract bracelet" in lieu of a wedding ring. This spectacular platinum bracelet was designed in the shape of a garter, and it had a cluster of cushion shaped sapphires in the center of a wide band of diamonds. This incredible piece was crafted in Paris by Van Cleef & Arpels. Going even further back in time, circa 1840, Prince Albert gave his betrothed, Queen Victoria, an engagement ring in the form of a serpent. Some say the serpent represented the ancient symbol of eternal love. Then for their sixth anniversary, Prince Albert lovingly gifted his wife a wreath for her hair. This wreath was made of porcelain and enameled gold, and it had an orange blossom motif on it, with a single orange blossom representing each of their children.

One should note that before the 19th century, engagement rings of any type for the bourgeoisie were uncommon. Prior to the Industrial Revolution, many people could not afford them. In fact, it was more typical in America at that time for a bride-to-be to receive a sewing thimble as a symbol of promise. It would be another 100 years before a diamond engagement ring would become popular. Again, thank you, De Beers.

By the way, it was also the brilliant marketing by De Beers that allowed them to tell consumers how much a man should spend on the engagement ring. It was fist suggested that a man should spend the equivalent of one month's salary on a proper promissory jewel. Several decades later, it became two month's salary. By 2010 (and perhaps due to economic hardships), these pricing methods were apparently no longer the standard measure. According to industry reports just few short years ago, the average engagement ring cost only a few thousand dollars.

So back to our initial question: how traditional do you want to be?

If we go back even further in history, say to the ancient Romans or Greeks, you'll find that women were given promissory bands. Sometimes the bands weren't gifted until the actual wedding ceremony, and the rings actually signified "ownership" rather than a promise of enduring and faithful love. Some bands were simple and made of gold, and some were simply made of iron.

A few hundred years later in the Byzantine era, marriage rings were still not a standard part of wedding ceremonies. In the instance when a ring would be created to symbolize the sacred union, it would be a simple gold band with a flat 'tablet' on top. This tablet might be inscribed or engraved with images and words, describing the sanctity of the marriage. Gemstones were not commonly used as decorative adornments in this type of jewelry.

We should also ask: where are you from?

Your heritage and geography will definitely affect your sense of "tradition" as well.

In some locations, such as in Germany, wedding rings are worn on the *right* hand instead of the left. The German tradition and belief is that the veins in the right hand are closer to the heart than in the left, so they opt to wear their wedding bands on their right hands. (The left hand tradition enjoyed in the USA is thought to originate from ancient Egyptian practice). Also, instead of rings, some societies prefer to give other types of jewelry, such as betrothal bracelets. And don't forget the older American 'tradition' of the sewing thimble!

So to sum it up: the most important thing is for brides to follow their hearts. If they want to call themselves 'traditional' based on the last century of popularity, a diamond engagement ring is lovely. Just be aware of where that "tradition" comes from. Conversely, many modern brides are looking for alternatives, not just in cost but also in uniqueness, collectability, and practicality. Colored exotic gemstones have a lot to offer in those areas as well, and many of these gems have alleged esoteric benefits, along with centuries of lore, that give these jewels genuine historical tradition.

Simply put – if there is a piece of jewelry that symbolizes your promise and enduring love for your betrothed, then that's the piece for you. Whether the jewelry has any diamonds in it, has any colored jewels, is simple or ornate, the point is: do it your way. Show your enduring love and devotion with a special symbol that speaks from your heart.

There are so many options with today's vast jewelry selections. Just find the one that represents you.

APPENDIX I

<u>Weights & Measures</u>

** An "a-ounce", as termed in this appendix, is what most people know as an "ounce." It's the standard unit of measure in many English speaking countries for weighing food. We use 'a-ounce' here as a shortened form of 'avoirdupois ounce,' and it distinguishes this common type of ounce from the *troy ounce* measure used internationally for weighing precious metals. **

Gold and Precious Metals are weighed by the Troy Ounce.

1 gram = 0.032151 troy ounces

1 gram = 0.035274 a-ounces
(where 16 a-ounces = 1 pound)

Conversely

1 a-ounce = 28.35 grams
1 pound = 453.6 grams
1 pound = 14.583 troy ounces

1 troy ounce = 31.1 grams
1 a-ounce = 28.35 grams

32.15 troy ounces = 1 kilogram

So what does this mean for you?

A troy ounce is heavier than the common ounce most of us are familiar with. Generally, a troy ounce weighs about 10% more than the standard ounce.

The everyday ounces most people are familiar with are the lighter weight, "avoirdupois ounces" – referred to above as the 'a-ounce.' The common "ounce" English speakers talk about is the avoirdupois ounce, from the avoirdupois system that we use to weigh food and our bodies. But when it comes to precious metals, the heavier troy ounce is the traditional and historical system of measure by which these metals are weighed and sold on the open market.

When you purchase one 'ounce' of gold, you're actually buying one "troy ounce."

Remember: one troy ounce is about 10% heavier than one a-ounce.

Often people want as much pure gold in their jewelry as they can get, and that is measured both by karat and by ounce weight. Many people assume that the heavier the metal, the more valuable the piece. That may or may not be the case; but it's likely true if you've purchased the most pure (closest to 100%) precious metal you can.

The first way to ensure that you're getting as much pure gold as possible, you should increase the karat weight of your jewelry. If you recall, 14k gold is only 58.5% pure gold; the remaining metal is an alloy used to give the gold added strength and durability. In comparison, 18k gold is 75% pure gold, whereas 24k gold is 100% pure gold. Pure gold is an extremely soft metal; and consequently, some alloy metal is normally mixed with pure gold to give your jewelry better durability and to protect and ensure its shape over the lifetime of the piece.

That said, assuming you have purchased the highest karat weight you can, the next unit of measurement is the jewelry's total weight in ounces. Depending on your scale and where you are in the world, you may hear jewelers talking in terms of 'grams' of gold. However, the standard for selling precious metals globally is in ounces…and more specifically, in troy ounces.

So how do you know whether you're getting, for example, a full troy ounce of gold in your jewelry? You must consider both the karat weight of your gold and the actual ounce weight of the metal.

Here's an example to help you calculate the amount of pure gold in any piece:

Example: You have an 18k gold pendant that weighs 25 grams.

How much pure gold (in troy ounces) do you have?

Calculate –

a) Convert gram weight to troy ounces:

25 grams = x troy ounces?

31.1 grams = 1 troy ounce

Convert gram weight to troy ounce weight:
25g/31.1g = .804 troy ounces

b) Determine purity of gold:

18k gold is 75% pure gold (= .75)

18k gold = .75 pure

c) Calculate the amount of pure gold based on total troy ounce weight in your piece:

.75 pure x .804 troy ounces = .603 troy ounces of pure gold

Answer: your 18k gold pendant that weighs 25 grams is actually .603 troy ounces of pure gold.

In using the various gram-to-ounce conversion equations listed above, and remembering to factor in the karat weight of your gold, you can estimate the actual troy ounce weight of pure gold in your jewelry by following the above example. Feel free to utilize a home scale or an inexpensive jewelry scale that uses gram weight measurements. From it, and by using the equations above, you can assess the amount of pure precious metal in your jewelry.

Then, if you want to estimate an approximate worth of your gold piece, you can multiply the current market price (per ounce of gold) times the troy ounce weight of gold. That will give you a baseline value to work with. Naturally, other factors will also affect the monetary worth of your jewelry – such as a designer name, a brand, artistry and craftsmanship, country of origin, age, etc.

FACTORING GEMSTONES INTO YOUR EQUATIONS

If you have jewelry with gemstones in it, or if you're a collector of loose gemstones, you need to consider the weight of your gem. To do so, the equation for estimating the weight of your gem is shown below. It's simple.

Once you estimate the gram weight of your gem, subtract it from the total gram weight of your jewelry piece to assess how much the metal alone weighs.

Gemstone Carat conversion to Gram Weight:

(note: do not confuse a gem's carat weight with gold's karat weight)

Measuring loose gemstones is not too different than measuring the weight of precious metals. It's simply a matter of knowing the proper equation for conversion.

There are several equations that can be used for conversion, but this is the simplest: multiply the gem's carat weight by 0.2 to get its equivalent gram weight –

Gem Carat Weight x 0.2 = gram weight

Ex: 4 carats x 0.2 = 0.8 grams

Ex: 5 carats x 0.2 = 1 gram

In short, 1 gram = 5 carats

Example

If you have a cocktail ring with a 3.5 carat gemstone, and its band is 14k gold; and the whole ring weighs 33 grams on your home scale, this is how you would estimate the weight of the gemstone and the weight of the pure gold (in troy ounces) in your ring:

a) Gemstone Conversion:
Carat Weight x 0.2 = gram weight of gem

3.5 carats x 0.2 = 0.7 grams

b) Gold Conversion:

14k gold ring = 58.5% pure gold

Ring weighs 33 grams: Subtract the gem weight (as calculated above) from the total weight of the ring:

33 grams – 0.7 grams = 32.3 grams of metal
(total ring) – (gem weight)   (metal weight alone)

Metal weight = 32.3 grams

c) Convert metal gram weight to troy ounce weight:
(remember: 31.1 grams = 1 troy ounce)

32.3g/31.1g = 1.04 troy ounces
(metal weight of ring)/(total grams in troy ounces) = total troy ounces in ring

d) Calculate the purity of your gold:
   1.04 troy ounces x .585 (14k = 58.5% pure)

<u>Answer:</u> .608 troy ounces of pure gold in your ring

** A note on pennyweights: 20 pennyweights = 1 troy ounce.

Oftentimes, the amount of pure gold in jewelry is so small that the preferred unit of measure to discuss the weight of the gold may be 'pennyweights.' It's an accepted universal way to refer to smaller amounts of gold, versus trying to say something weighs 1/20th of a troy ounce.

ABOUT THE AUTHOR

Christine Cameron starred for years as the host of her own national jewelry television show. Her industry niche is luxury teleshopping, and her specialty is exotic and high-jewelry. She was also a product buyer, a TV Talent trainer, and a liaison to jewelry manufacturers all around the globe. Her experience in the jewelry and TV industries has allowed her to develop relationships with some of the world's most talented lapidaries (gemstone cutters) and designers. To date, she has appeared on four American TV networks as a Show Host and Jewelry Expert.

Using her blend of skills and knowledge, Christine also contracts with GIA to develop content for them. Her GIA projects are on-going and, understandably, cannot be discussed until they are published. Suffice to say that her expertise is used to enlighten and entertain jewelry lovers, young and old, both novice and expert, in the world of exquisite jewels.

Additionally, Christine spent many years as the EVP of Sales and Marketing for an international business. And currently she lends her talents to a crop of young, aspiring fashionistas as an Adjunct Professor. In 2011, she earned her Masters degree in Entertainment Business and graduated Summa Cum Laude with many honors. She was also Valedictorian of her class.

Christine has written both editions of SAVVY as a leading consumer advocate for jewelry lovers. She hopes to illuminate, educate, and clarify for the savvy shopper what true value is in today's crowded jewelry marketplace. With so many manufacturers hawking their goods, how do you know a truly valuable piece from something that has been altered or manipulated to look good?

Christine hopes you will gain incredible insight and confidence by reading SAVVY; and she invites you to join her at one of her live seminars or in one of her online classes. You can find her schedule at savvygems.com, or you can inquire about her trunk shows and speaking opportunities at savvyswagbag.com.

Her background is solid, her expertise with exotic gemstones is exceptional, her eye for detail is extraordinary, and her approach to sharing this knowledge with you is nothing but common sense.

Christine's high-jewelry and exotic gemstone TV shows have been broadcast on the Gem Shopping Network, America's Value Channel, Today's Shopping Network, and the Ultimate Shopping Network.

Whether you plan to purchase jewelry in a store, at a trunk show, as swag, online, or on television, Christine's tricks of the trade are sure to make you a savvy jewelry and gemstone connoisseur...overnight!

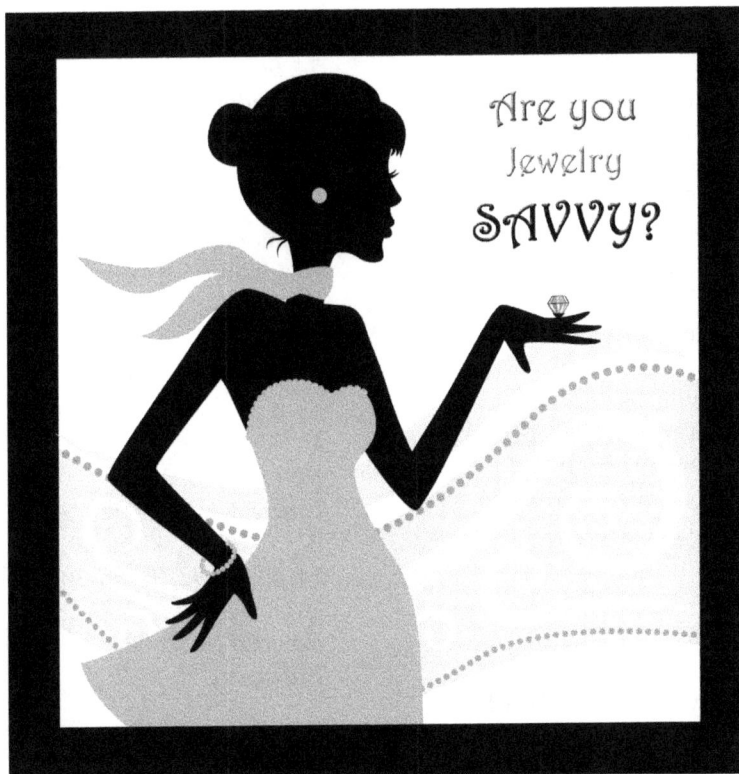

www.savvygems.com

Swag Bags
Trunk Shows
Designer Discounts
And More…

Your Discount Code: **2SAVVY**

christine@savvygems.com

INDEX

I
Inclusion, 36-37, 84
Intrinsic Value, 5, 6, 8, 9, 15
Iolite, 38, 90, 92, 95
Iridescence, 23

J
Jade, 25, 46, 54, 56, 75, 90, 91
Jasper, 54, 90, 96
Jet, 48

K
Kashmir Sapphire, 5, 8, 26, 32, 56-57, 104
Kunzite, 95

L
Labradorite, 23, 96
Lapis Lazuli, 47, 54, 77, 90, 91, 96
Larimar, 48

M
Malachite, 48, 97
Marquise cut, ii, 86, 87
Mohs Scale, 93-94
Moonstone, 22, 47, 75, 89, 96
Morganite, 40-41, 89, 95
Mother of Pearl, 23, 38, 67
Mystic Topaz, 18-19

O
Obsidian, 48
Onyx, 54, 91, 96
Opal, 23, 51, 67, 75-76, 89, 90, 91, 96, 102
Oval cut, ii, 87

P
Padparadscha, 8, 32, 53, 78-79
Palladium, 59-68
Pearl, 23, 51, 76-77, 89, 91, 92, 97
Pearose cut, ii
Pennyweight, 115
Peridot, 38, 77, 90, 91, 96
Phenomena, 22-23, 31
Pink Diamond, 4-5, 26, 57
Platinum, 59-68
Prasiolite, 40, 47, 89, 96
Precious Metals, 15, 58, 59-68,
Precious (stones), 31
Princess cut, ii, 86, 87

Q
Quartz, 22, 23, 41, 47, 94, 96

R
Radiant Square cut, ii
Rarity, 24-25, 30, 31, 58
Rhodium, 17, 59-68
Rhodochrosite, 8, 25, 26, 45, 56, 77, 97
Ruby, 8, 22, 25, 32, 37, 53, 56, 77, 89, 91, 92, 94, 95, 98, 102-103, 108

S
Sapphire, 5, 8, 16, 17, 18, 23, 25, 26, 32, 37, 54, 56, 69, 77-79, 89-90, 91, 92, 94, 95, 103, 107
Scarcity, 24-25, 30
Semi-Precious, 31, 37-41
Silver, 59-68, 92

SAVVY